To
Sholom
Estrin

Sept 3rd. 2015
Emory

ARYAN PAPERS

George Dyrin

ARYAN PAPERS

GEORGE DYNIN

ARCHWAY
PUBLISHING

Archway Publishing books may be ordered through booksellers or by contacting:

Archway Publishing
1663 Liberty Drive
Bloomington, IN 47403
www.archwaypublishing.com
1-(888)-242-5904

ISBN: 978-1-4808-1137-9 (sc)
ISBN: 978-1-4808-1138-6 (hc)
ISBN: 978-1-4808-1139-3 (e)

Library of Congress Control Number: 2014917009

Printed in the United States of America.

Archway Publishing rev. date: 10/02/2014

This book is dedicated to my heroic mother, Fania

and to

Jan and Halina Plater-Zyberk, who helped us during the
worst time of our lives without considering their own.

There is no such thing as a hopeless situation.

The days are frightening. It is like Hell reigns all over the World.

You are in fear of your life each moment.
You watch your words and gestures.
What is said is important.
It can give a clue who you are.
You are a walking mask.
Your life restarts during the night. You may dream sweet dreams.
You are in a normal world—you are in paradise.
The night is passing fast. You hope it will last forever.
You hope you will wake up and think:
What a terrible dream was the day. Let's live in night!

George Dynin

FOREWORD

by Sir Martin Gilbert

GEORGE DYNIN'S MEMOIR IS a tribute to hope and education. The hope is that of a young Jew caught up in the Holocaust; the education is the knowledge of the realities of the Holocaust in all its manifestations: suffering, courage, escape, rescue, resistance, and above it all—powerfully illustrated in this book—survival.

Born in the Polish industrial city of Lodz in 1925, George Dynin gives a charming portrayal of pre-war Jewish life. With the coming of war begins the first of four remarkable journeys, each of them mapped in this book. The first journey was in search of a safe haven from the German military advance into Poland; that journey took him to Vilna, in independent Lithuania. There, safety was followed first by Soviet and then by German rule, leading to the second journey, deep into Belarus, and a life in hiding, masquerading as a Christian. The third journey, after liberation, is to Vilna and back to Lodz. The fourth journey is from Lodz to British Mandate Palestine.

There are many powerful and thought-provoking episodes in these pages. The German air bombardments in the first days of the war are described with a terrifying immediacy. So is the Soviet deportation of Jews from Vilna. And the first days of the German occupation of Vilna. The fears and perils of life in the countryside, first in Lithuania and then in Belarus, with the ever-present danger of discovery, betrayal, and arrest, are powerfully conveyed: they are a theme of this story, as are the helping hands offered by those Christians whose own lives were at risk should their "gentile" guests be unmasked. Some of the most moving passages describe when George Dynin is in church, having to pass himself off as a devout Christian.

Every story of survival is different. George Dynin's account adds a vivid and inspiring dimension to what we know about Jews who survived with an Aryan identity. How to avoid being seized with other Poles for forced labour in Germany? George's mother had the answer: she signed him up for work in the forest as a logger, out of sight of the German occupiers. "This was the first physical labor of my life," he comments. Danger and death were everywhere; one day, George and his mother heard the shots of an automatic when fifteen young Jewish men and women were executed. "A few minutes later, we heard another discharge. Then a few single shots. It was horrible. We realized that these shots served to kill off the miserable young lives." George writes, *"They're killing innocent people over there,* I said to God, rather than to myself or to Mother."

Every page of this book brings those horrendous years into sharp focus through the eyes of a human and thoughtful young man, whose decision to write his memoirs is a gain to all those who want to try to understand human nature, in all its variety.

When the German occupiers were driven out of eastern Poland, George and his mother made their way to Vilna, where she worked as a secretary in a weather station and George as a student-baker. Their search to find George's father, who had been in the Soviet Union during the war, was rewarded when a telegram arrived from Moscow, reporting that "Father was in one piece in Palestine; that was our new goal." This they did, with George serving as a soldier in Israel's War of Independence. For the survivors, Jewish life was renewed; one of the uplifting photographs in this book is of George with his parents and his sister, sitting in a coffeehouse in Tel-Aviv.

PREFACE

I BEGAN TO WRITE these memoirs in the last months of 1946 in Tel-Aviv under the British mandate. It was a fulfillment of a vow I had made during the war: I had promised God that I would write a book-memoir in which I would depict the war experiences of my family. My conscience deemed this promise necessary. I shall then attempt to represent the world I saw, a world of falsity and hypocrisy, patriotism and treason. I shall also show how, due to circumstances, my family's experiences differ from those of the other Jews who survived on "Aryan" papers.

I shall devote much space to my inner transformations for they are not common. I shall describe the wisdom and the folly of particular people who played a part in this bloody drama. I shall try to portray henchmen, informants, traitors, but also the people who helped us, risking their own lives and the lives of their families. I believe that the atrocities we witnessed and about which we heard must be preserved in writing so that the future generations can be aware of them.

I begin an immense task without any certainty that I can accomplish it. It may be beyond my strength; nonetheless, I wish to describe the immeasurable evils and blessings of that time. I want to describe that horrific life, but at this very moment I feel so feeble that I doubt my own ability to do it. But just like in those dark days, so now too I may experience God's help, for which I pray. May God endow me with inspiration and talent. Unfortunately, I have not foreseen that conditions of life and the passage of time can change a man so. During the war I was forced to ponder things and to ask myself the most penetrating questions. But as I wrote these memoirs during short breaks from hard labor, it was impossible for me to delve deeply into my soul again. Hence certain moments which I had promised myself to write down have eluded me: I have not been able to recapture them with absolute precision. I did not know this then, just as I did not know that I would break yet another promise given to God, one incommensurate with my physical development at the time.

ACKNOWLEDGMENTS

WITHOUT THE INPUT OF my wife, Dr. Marlene Kemp-Dynin, this book would never have been published. I thank her for the countless hours that she spent on editing and technical matters, as well as for her support.

I am extremely grateful to Sir Martin Gilbert for encouraging me to publish my book and for providing me with his Foreword and maps.

I would like to thank all the people who read my manuscript for their positive critiques and comparisons to books that had been awarded the Nobel Prize in Literature.

And I would like to thank the Almighty for giving me the chance to see my book published during my lifetime.

PROLOGUE

I WAS BORN IN the city of Lodz, in central Poland, on March 19, 1925. I attended kindergarten on Gdanska Street, not far from my home. On the corner house, just a short walk from the kindergarten, were attached two large signs advertising two doctors, both Lichtensteins, husband and wife, with offices on the second floor. They were the parents of my classmate Tolek. Their apartment was on the same floor, and many times after school, we went there to play. Mietek Rosen and another boy named Padwa were also my friends from the kindergarten. Later, all four of us started elementary school together and continued with Gimnazjum Spoleczne—which was High School—on Pomorska Street.

The owner/director of the kindergarten, Mrs. Paszkowna, was a nice lady who was dedicated to teaching us ballet, French, art, etc. I still have a few photos showing me performing ballet in one of the children's stories, for the benefit of invited parents. Each of the students was assigned a black sticker in the shape of an animal. I felt as though I was tops in the school, as my animal was … the lion. It was proudly attached to my open wardrobe locker.

My best friend at this time was a boy named Marek Arkusz, who lived one floor above our apartment on Andrzeja. His full name translated from Polish was "sheet of stamps," which was a little funny.

Marek was a student in the Hebrew School—it was the very best school in town and on the same level as Gimnazjum Spoleczne. Each time we met, we played chess. As we met every day, I started to be highly specialized in chess and beat all my opponents, except for my father, who was a chess genius.

When I was about four and a half years old, I had the typical Polish haircut called "grzywka," a short, straight cut. I always wore a blue beret. I remember that one time, my parents were talking about the bad health of my paternal grandfather, Moses. He lived with my grandmother, Musia, in an apartment at 8 Sierpnia Street. The outside of the house was dark from pollution caused by the air of industrial Lodz. My father took me upstairs, and the maid opened the door. He entered the room, and I was asked to wait outside. A few minutes later, I joined him. The following is vivid in my memory. My grandfather was lying on the bed. He stretched out his hand to me to be kissed, which I did reluctantly. This was the last time I saw Moses alive. The next time, all I saw was his cemetery lot with a large granite monument. His name and other details were inscribed on it. That was during my visit to Vienna in 1999. The monument was like new, without a scratch. I declared it as a survivor of the Holocaust. Sometime after Moses had died, Grandmother Musia moved to our apartment at 11 Listopada.

Jadzia, our live-in maid, was one of the occupants of our modest apartment on Andrzeja Street. When the weather allowed, she took me for a long walk to Park Poniatowski. In the park, we always passed the white-painted bridge over a huge fish pond in the middle of the park. I had bread to feed the fish with me. I liked to observe them grabbing the bread. I imagined that, in the pond, there were huge fish, much larger than the one I could see. Afterward, we continued to walk in the direction of the train station. I was fascinated with locomotives, and I loved the trains that were passing through. At that time, the locomotives spilled a lot of smoke and steam and made great noises. I was always very happy with these almost-daily strolls, and so was Jadzia, who was able to meet her boyfriend. Each time, he was waiting for her next to the railroad station on the edge of Park Poniatowski.

I adored my grandparents Leon and Ethel. I probably liked Leon even better than Ethel. They lived a few houses from ours. Each weekend, I carried my pajamas to their house and spent the night. The next morning, I would go with my grandfather to his property on Zielony Rynek. He rented this area to people who sold herrings, other fish, vegetables, and so forth, and each week, he collected rent from these tenants. They paid with coins, as there were high denominations of coins in Poland, and paper money was not much in use for such small transactions like buying a herring. We returned home with bags of coins, very heavy and smelling of herring and other fish. At home, we put all the bags on the table, sorted the coins, and counted the entire lot. For it, I always got some small cash. I earned this money. When I went home, I still smelled of herrings. But I was proud of it.

My life was quite good. I was adored by all my family from both sides. For many years, I was without competition. This didn't last forever. Nine years after I was born, my parents presented me with a cute little sister. Her name was Aviva Marcela. She was born soon after my father came back from a trip to Palestine, and the name Aviva was very appropriate. Aviva means "spring," and she was born in May. In a matter of days, another newcomer arrived. Her name was Maya, and she was the daughter of Rachel, my beloved aunt and the sister of my mother. So we were now three. Still, since I was a boy and the firstborn, I held an advantage among the younger generation of our family. I was probably a good-looking boy, as strangers on the street stopped and said, "What a nice boy!" Yes, I was definitely keeping a "winning distance" from the my newborn "competitors."

During my early years, we always spent the summer at a nearby resort, a rather modest place named "Zielona Gora." Later, when my father acquired more wealth, we traveled farther to Ciechocinek, famous for its mineral waters; to Muszyna and Krynica in the mountains; and to Orlowo on the shores of the Baltic Sea. I remember each of these locations for different reasons. Zielona Gora I remember because I rode a horse for the first time in my life, and I was scared to death. The horse was definitely too big for my first experience. I was so happy to be back with my two feet on the ground. Ciechocinek was very popular with my family, and we were there many times. We always rented a quarter of the same villa, while three other families rented the rest of the villa. There were always children my age to play with. I remember the first year in Ciechocinek because of the young girls I was touching—and by whom I was kissed in return. As time progressed, I was more and more interested in the opposite sex. One summer, the total of four families in the villa included one girl and three boys. The parents of the girl invited all three of us to their farm near the border with Germany. They were well-to-do and had a sugar factory in this huge farm. The girl's name was Krysia. She had long, dark hair, was very nice, and spoke very warmly and slowly. All three of us were instantly in love with her. She, of course, figured it out and teased us accordingly, kissing each of us on the mouth for good measure.

Across the road from our villa was a coffeehouse named "Pod Wieza." Translated this means "under the tower." The coffeehouse was so named because there was a huge water tower next to it. Live music was supplied by a group named "Karasinski i Kataszek," well-known Warsaw musicians. Live music was fantastic, and I loved it. I had very good relations with the musicians, and, therefore, they let me sit next to the orchestra during performances, which I enjoyed tremendously. Soon after, I started to compose some melodies in my head. My father visited us on the weekends, and we all went to the large coffeehouse called "On the Swimming Pool", to enjoy what was known as "five o-clock." Here again was not only great music, but also fantastic ice cream.

Orlowo, on the Baltic Sea, I remember not only because of the daughter of our summer landlord, but also because I collected each day small pieces of amber on the beach, and, from time to time, I caught some beautiful rainbow trout in the mountain-like stream next to our home. From time to time, we visited Sopot and walked the entire length of the beautiful sea pier.

Muszyna, where we spent our last summer before the war, was the most exiting in my memories. I was friendly with a girl named Mary, who was a few years older than me. We climbed the hills, drank water from mountain springs and crystal-clear streams, and she introduced me to her beautiful anatomy. But not much more. Yes, it was definitely the best vacation I had before the war. When I was back in Lodz after liberation, I sent a letter to Mary. I didn't know either her last name or her address. I sent it to Muszyna, describing the location of her home and addressed it simply to Mary. The letter was delivered, and we exchanged correspondence for some time.

Next to Muszyna was Krynica. One year, my grandmother Musia was spending her summer in this beautiful mountain resort. I remember vividly bicycling from Muszyna to Krynica and back to visit my grandmother. The view from the road was gorgeous. The highway was hilly, and it was a very difficult task to bicycle there. In some places it was impossible to ride, and I had to walk next to my bicycle. But I never gave up, and I made it back to Muszyna in one piece. I was proud of myself.

Upon entering high school (gimnazium), all students were required to wear school uniforms—no exceptions. The housekeeper of the school stood at the entrance gate, and students without uniforms were not admitted to the building. I remember the tailor who made my uniform. His name was Migdal. His workshop was located in a small wooden house, painted green, on Gdanska Street. I was always a little scared when he was pulling out my sleeves, which were partly attached to the rest of uniform. He did it in one fast and strong movement, and it was always accompanied by a tearing noise.

Gimnazjum Spoleczne was a no-nonsense school. Lack of attention was not tolerated. The teachers were picked from the best in Lodz— except for one. His name was Landecki. His original name was Landau, before he converted from Judaism to Catholicism. I do not know why he decided to hate me. As a result of his hatred, I was always afraid of him. His method was very sadistic. He called me to the blackboard and tried to trick me into giving him a wrong answer. During one lesson, his question about classical Greece was: where is the Peloponnese? He knelt on the floor next to the large map of Greece in order to reach some other part of Greece than the Peloponnese and pretended that he was helping me to find it. I pointed at the spot he suggested, and the entire class laughed, including Landecki. From that time on, I was called "Peloponnese" by my classmates.

The lessons I liked the best were physics, mathematics, and particularly nature. The last one was taught by a young female teacher, Mrs. Bielska. She was just great. During her lessons, everybody concentrated on her every word. Each year, we had two weeks of her lessons at a country estate located near the river Pilica, a few hours by bus from the school. The sleeping accommodation was simple but very clean, and the food was very good. Small lakes were abundant around us, and some ruins of an old castle were nearby; there, we caught various lizards. There was one microscope for each student, and with them, we looked at various slides, mostly with drops of water from ponds in the area. Each drop was like an ocean of life.

Our teacher of Polish was a writer/poet who wrote under the name of Jastrun and was well-known in Poland. He was the husband of our great nature teacher. I liked his lessons about famous Polish writers, like Sienkiewicz, the poet Mickiewicz, and others. I learned that both teachers had survived the war; he, like the majority of students, was Jewish. In our class, thirty students were Jewish and four were Christian. Most students came from Lodz's snobbish families. The school was extremely expensive and very patriotic. A few times a week, we met after five in the afternoon at our homes to play table soccer with various sizes of buttons for the class championship. After one of us finally claimed the championship, we started a new championship, this time bridge. I learned three years ago that my classmates from Gimnazjum Spoleczne who survived the war and are living now in Israel are still meeting to play bridge.

My father became richer and richer with passing time. Once, we had a new white Mercedes with red leather interior and a roof that opened. Sometimes I asked the chauffeur, Mr. Mitchnik, to open the roof, and then I stood in the car mimicking a well-known German dictator. Passing through the streets of my town Lodz, I was rather proud that people looked at me with curiosity. My relations with our chauffeurs were always the best possible for obvious reasons. I liked their stories and their well-pressed uniforms. Every time they passed our maid, Mary, they hugged her intensely.

I had a great-uncle living in Zgierz not far from Lodz. His brother, my grandfather Leon, took me a number of times to visit him. We always took the tramway from Lodz to go there. My great-uncle had a hardware store. He was a very nice man and tried to make me happy on each visit. He always offered me tools from his store to take with me and asked me to come again. I liked him. One day, my great-uncle died. The family decided to bury him in Lodz and not in Zgierz for reasons unknown to me. Apparently it was very complicated at that time to bring the deceased from one city to another. Therefore, my father decided to bring the body to Lodz in our car. Since the police sometimes checked cars entering Lodz and because it was illegal to transport a dead person in a private car, the poor great-uncle was placed, fully-dressed, in a sitting position on the backseat between our chauffer and an employee from my father's business. My uncle Siomek was the driver. The trip went without problems. At that time I was very upset; however, later I found the episode to be rather funny.

I was not always a total angel. When I was ten years old, I prepared a plastic bag with water and tiptoed into the accounting department of my father's business. A very fat lady named Ania Bernstein worked there. I moved close to her, and, in the split second before she sat down at the typewriter, I tossed the bag with water on the chair. It was very successful in my mind. The bag exploded and water splashed all over. Ania was completely wet. As a result, I was unceremoniously thrown out of the office by clerks and soon after spanked by my father without mercy.

Curiosity is probably common in eleven-year-olds. I was definitely always curious about why my uncle Siomek, my mother's brother, brought his young female visitors to his room and then closed the door and locked it with the key. I decided to have a closer look to solve this question. My closer look was directed at the keyhole. The keys at that time were big, and so was the keyhole. What I found was my first lesson in human reproduction. I decided that this could be very interesting for me as well. I decided to go to the service room of Magda, the maid of my grandparents, and I explained to her what I had seen in Siomek's room. I asked her if she would like to do the same with me. The answer was like a cold shower: "You are still too young for it." I asked how long I should wait. No answer was forthcoming, and I was nicely asked to leave the room.

There are some small episodes from my childhood that shall stay in my memory forever. I remember a small boy, Julek Bialostocki, from my third grade of elementary school. He sat on the front bench in our classroom, was always neatly dressed, and had short blond hair and big blue eyes. One day, he was absent from class. The next day, our teacher was crying and surprised us by telling us that Julek had died in the hospital from appendicitis. I remember that there was a short, indescribable noise in the classroom and then complete silence. I couldn't comprehend that, just two days before, Julek had been sitting there, not very far from me, and now he had just disappeared—vanished. I just couldn't bear it! I looked from time to time at his empty bench. Some moments I felt that I still saw him. The entire class went to his funeral. We all wore black armbands. This was my first meeting with death. Until this time, I didn't know the real meaning of death. I simply never thought about it. Immediately, I started to imagine some specific smell of death. I smelled it in the cemetery and for a long time in our third-grade classroom. I remember Julek Bialostocki from my childhood even now, after so many years. I can still see him sitting on the first bench with his short blond hair and his big blue eyes. Amen.

I will never forget my bar mitzvah. I will never forget the ceremony in the synagogue. As my father always supported philanthropic causes, he decided that my bar mitzvah would take place in an "Altheim," a home for old and poor men, located on Pomorska Street. The building was built from red bricks and was in drastic need of refurbishing. Bar mitzvahs were the source of income of this institution. When I entered the synagogue, which was located on the main floor of the building, and climbed to the podium, the "bema," I looked around, and all I could see were old men, in black attire, with long beards, who were looking at me. The worst part was an indescribable smell mixing with the aroma of the kosher goodies that had been laid on a long table. I forgot temporarily where I was and what I should do. Somehow, the rabbi gave me a light poke in the ribs, and I started to read the prescribed part. Afterward, I was asked to sit at the table with food, and everybody was drinking "L'chaim" with a red sweet wine. When I got home, my room was full of assorted gifts, like books, games, boxing gloves, and so forth. I was very happy to receive so many gifts from my large family, friends, clerks from our business, and from others. At that time, I did not know that I would part with all of my treasures very soon.

I must end these episodes from my childhood by imagining that my mother is playing her beloved Grieg sonatas. When she played, I always sat next to her piano, absorbing each note she played. I begged her not to stop and to play more and more. She played so beautifully. It felt as if an army of shivers were passing through my body. These were the most pleasant and remembered episodes of my childhood. These were irreplaceable moments, lost forever, except when reborn in my memory.

"From Childhood to September 1, 1939"
Kindergarten "Paszkowna" on Gdanska Street in Lodz
I am the upper-left "flower"

"My first date"
Wisniowa Gora near Lodz
Summer 1930

With my grandparents, Leon and Ethel
Krynica mountain resort
1931

With my Aunt Rachel (second from left) and her girlfriends
Time and place unknown

On the boat on the Baltic Sea with my grandmother Ethel
Gdynia, 1936

Last photo before the war
I am wearing the official school uniform and am with my mother
Summer 1939

My sister, Aviva Marcela
Her nickname was "Dzidzia"
1938 or 1939

Maya and Aviva during a birthday party; they
were born almost on the same date
Maya was our first cousin, the daughter of Rachel, our mother's sister
Lodz, time unknown

Maya—her last photo before the war
She was killed in Treblinka in 1942

Small family gathering in our home in Lodz
Date unknown
From left to right:
Ethel Glowinski, my maternal grandmother; killed in Treblinka in 1942
Cela Dynin, the wife of Jona; killed in the
Holocaust, place and time unknown
Mietek Chigryn, the husband of Rachel; died in Bergen
Belsen a few days before liberation on April 11, 1945
My mother (standing); survived the Holocaust with me and my sister
Rachel Chigryn, my aunt; killed in Treblinka in 1942
Dr. Jona Dynin, my uncle and brother of my
father; killed during the Holocaust
Not in this photo:
My father, David; arrested by the Soviet police and sent from Wilno
to Siberia just before the Germans occupied Wilno; survived the war
Musia Dynin, David's mother; died in the Lodz Ghetto
Leon Glowinski, my maternal grandfather; killed in Treblinka in 1942
Sioma Glowinski, my mother's brother. Survived the
war by running away from Kaunus, Lithuania, where
he worked before the German Occupation

CHAPTER ONE

WHEN I LOOKED OUT the window after the air raid, I saw that the house across the street had been partly destroyed. It was a strange feeling. I wondered whether there were any people there. This was my first encounter with near death. I felt an emptiness invading my heart, and I did not fully realize what had happened. I had to look that way again and again to ascertain that it was not my imagination. It was not clear to me why I had to keep checking; after all, it was obvious that the house was in ruins. This was my very first image of the war, and as such, I wanted to push it away. Then I asked another question: What if a bomb falls on our house as well, and we share the fate of the people who used to live across the street? This is how I came to know the fear of death.

During the air raids that followed, we went down to a shelter, or rather a cellar prepared especially for that purpose. There, we found several wounded tenants from the house across the street. One of them, Mr. Vova, an acquaintance of ours, had the most pitiful bearing. He sat against the wall, breathing heavily, his head covered in bandages. As I found out later, he was in shock. Others had more superficial cuts. No one who had been gravely wounded was in the cellar; they had been taken directly to the hospital. The air smelled powerfully of iodine and valerian. The floor next to the first-aid kit, where the wounded had been dressed, was stained with blood. Among the victims was a woman whose face was terribly cut by glass; hers was the first blood I saw during the war.

From then on, we slept in the shelter. Actually, we spent almost all of our time in the shelter because, during the day, there were new alerts every other minute. I remember that, in the morning, the milkman brought milk as usual, but everyone bought two liters instead of the customary one, and all of the milk was gone in no time. They would say, "It's war time. One must buy things when they're still there; later on they might be unavailable."

I remembered my grandmother's stories about famine during the Great War. One of the women in the shelter helped me understand the gravity of the situation when she told my mother that she would exchange her diamond ring for bread in order to feed her child. On the third day of the war, the radio announced, "Gas alarm for the zone P.Z. 10," and soon thereafter, "Gas alarm for the zone Lodz. Enemy pilots drop test tubes with bacteria as well as explosive candy and toys."

"The end must be near," said some. "The Germans want to test the Blitzkrieg on us." We prepared our gas masks. Someone suggested that the best protection was a cotton ball dipped in urine and held close to the face. A lady with a small Doberman pinscher was already preparing for a gas attack. She held cotton saturated with a liquid from a bottle first in front of her face, then in front of the dog's snout. This looked hilarious, despite the seriousness of the situation, and later on, when we were in a safe place, we laughed to tears remembering that scene.

Several women, including our servant Regina, knelt in front of the painting of the Madonna and, in a flood of tears, recited litanies. Father wanted us to return to the apartment because he believed it made more sense to be higher up, because of the possible use of gas. On the way from the shelter to the apartment, I tried not to breathe at all to avoid the bacteria purportedly deployed by the Germans. I thought that they could penetrate into my lungs with the outside air. The alarm, however, was called off before we made it to the apartment. All our fear was for nothing because, as it turned out, there had been no gas or bacteria. My soul lightened up when I heard this. The danger moved away from me, and I had felt it so very close. That night, I slept in our apartment. It was our last night at home, the last night before wandering off into the unknown.

The following day, the Germans were already in Piotrkow. Father decided that we would not stay in the city. For several hours, we discussed various possibilities of escape. We talked about renting a bus to get to Rowne, but we had to abandon this idea because of insufficient fuel. The remaining options were to use our or my uncle's car. At the time, we owned a white convertible Mercedes, which stood in the garage with a freshly charged battery. Father had gotten it ready when he heard of the approaching war. "I want the car to be in order so that the army can use it," he had said, certain that cars would be confiscated at once. That did not happen, however, and the car was at our disposal. In addition to securing enough fuel, we had to obtain a pass called an "evacuational" because, if we traveled without it, the army could indeed seize the vehicle. That particular pass was not easy to get. Hundreds of people stood in line, while the person responsible for their issuance did not bother to hurry. On our behalf, a friend obtained it with great difficulty by paying a one-thousand-zloty bribe. It was a lot of money then, but no one minded spending that much in order to escape the Germans and the approaching front.

We began packing at once. Only that which was absolutely indispensable could be taken along. I packed my own belongings. Priceless treasures remained behind in the armoire: a postal stamp collection, a beautiful set of games, boxing gloves with a punching bag, etc. Naturally, I was very attached to all these objects, but at that moment, they were useless to me because they were not practical. I left behind all of my little and great belongings, and when I took a few steps with the suitcase in my hand, I turned to look back. The armoire was open. From its interior my favorite books called out to me; the toys of my childhood beckoned; my clothes, including the school uniform, all made to measure by the best tailor in town, Mr. Migdal, looked dejectedly at me. Brand-new ski boots, which I had not used even once, were on the floor.

I wanted to pick them up and take them along when Miss Hania, my cousin Majusia's nanny, entered the room. Her eyes paused on the boots. "If you want to leave them, I'll take them," she said. "My shoes are not strong enough for the escape out of town."

Needless to say, I gave them to her at once. Oh, how the open armoire still attracts my eyes. The five volumes of the *World and Life* encyclopedia seemed to be saying, "How so? You abandon us and will never again look at our pictures?" I waved them away and stepped out of the room, to re-enter it only six years later.

By the time we were ready to leave, it was quite dark. All of our family gathered in the apartment: Grandpa, two Grandmas, and Aunt Rysia with her husband and their little daughter Majusia. We were supposed to send a car to fetch them as soon as we reached Warsaw, our first stop. Without the slightest nervousness, I got into the car. I did not and could not realize what was ahead of me. I did not realize that I might be leaving my family home and my beloved city forever. I left without experiencing any of those feelings.

In the car, there was very little room: instead of four, there were six people. I was down on the floor in the back, while my legs rested on the neck of the passenger in front of me. Uncle Sioma was driving. Whenever I tried to adjust my uncomfortable position, there were voices of protest on all sides, above all from Mr. Vova, on whose neck I kept my feet. We drove through the city with dimmed lights. At the city gates, we were asked for the pass, and we got onto the road to Warsaw. Near Lowicz, next to a bridge, we were stopped by a soldier, who told us to continue slowly and to keep to the left, "because on the bridge there are unexploded German bombs." I was very scared, and only once we had crossed the bridge did I breathe with relief. The others calmed down as well.

We crossed a little town; the train depots were on fire. Somewhere in the distance, we saw a glow: Sochaczew. We got out of the car to stretch out. The grown-ups began discussing a place to spend the night. Afraid of night air raids, they wanted to sleep somewhere on the road so that we would arrive in Warsaw in the morning. Then we would send the car back to Lodz to fetch the rest of the family. We asked one of the local people about accommodation for the night. He looked at us with surprise: "You want to spend the night here, and the front is just around the corner, forty kilometers away."

We were all exhausted by the nerve-wracking journey. It was out of the question for my uncle, the most tired of all of us, to turn back to get the rest of the family. This made me glad; I was afraid that the car might not come back, and we might be stuck here. *Oh, to go on, as far as possible from the approaching front,* I thought, without remembering my beloved Grandpa, Grandmas, and Aunt Rysia. I was not thinking of them; I only wanted to save myself. *As for them, whatever happens, happens; they will somehow make it through,* I deceived myself. This was my first and only inhumanity during the war. It never happened again. In that moment, the war made the worst in me come to the surface: my egoism.

We arrived in Warsaw during the night and stopped at the home of my father's cousin, Rachel. The day was rather calm. The sirens hardly stopped, but there were few real air raids. High up, we could see German planes shot at by the Zenith anti-aircraft guns. We did not go to the shelter, and while carelessly standing by the window, I could see a plane that lowered itself suddenly and dropped a bomb on the nearby railway station. Father and Uncle Sioma went out to look for gas. In the meantime, the car was in the garage next door, where they were installing a special baggage rack on the roof. From now on, we were going to travel more comfortably.

The road from Warsaw to Minsk Mazowiecki was crowded. Several lanes of cars moved—or rather tried to move along. Everybody was honking, and the resulting sound resembled a prolonged wail. It was very difficult to make our way through this confusion. The drivers cursed each other. For an unknown reason, one of them, in the uniform of a lieutenant, threatened that he would shoot through our tires. The road from Minsk to Siedlce was somewhat less packed.

Siedlce. We were just outside the town. We had passed the woods full of deep craters, traces of the air raids. We had crossed forests filled with soldiers and reservists. At last, we had arrived at the town square. The men, as was now the usual practice, began searching for gas. There were rumors that the mayor issued five liters per person, which was a significant help for us as it was impossible to buy gas privately. My mother, my sister, and I entered the first little restaurant we saw to get something to eat. We had not yet finished our tea when I noticed that the people in the street were running chaotically, shouting, "Alarm, alarm!" Presently the characteristic *voom, voom, voom* of the German planes reached our ears. The anti-aircraft guns were silent, perhaps not there at all. We heard the first whiz of the falling bomb, then felt its impact. The people in the restaurant all crowded into a little hallway that gave onto the courtyard. It was a crush, but I felt safer there and did not realize that it would not matter which side of the house we were on.

The sound of falling bombs became clearer and clearer, and the house in which we were standing—wooden, one story high—began to sway in all directions. Of course, none of the window panes were left. With every whiz of a falling bomb, we instinctively bent down; as the bombs became more and more frequent, we remained bent over almost the whole time. Mother held me and my sister tightly. We held each other, convinced that every coming bomb was the one that would hit the house. All the while I recited the saying "not for a dog is the sausage; not for the cat is the lard," deeply believing that, if I managed to say it all between two falling bombs, they would not hit us. Such was my defense.

Suddenly, a horrific whiz just above our heads: This is the end. I closed my eyes. We held on to each other with all our strength. This lasted only a few seconds, but it was awful. A large bomb landed on the house across the street; pieces of walls fell on us and on others. A pillar of fresh smoke appeared above the city. When we left the restaurant, there were fires burning in the street, and the dead and the wounded were being carried on stretchers. I will never forget the face of the dead orderly who was being carried on a stretcher by two fellow orderlies. This was the first corpse I saw during the war—the first one I had seen in my life.

Soon father appeared, and Uncle Sioma and Mr. Vova followed

shortly. They recounted their experiences in a hurry. During the raid, Sioma was filling up the gas tank, and despite the falling bombs, he did not stop for fear that there would be no more gas to be had. He complained bitterly about the man who dispensed gas unhurriedly, without minding the hundreds of people who were waiting in line for this sole source of gas in the whole town of Siedlce. We could barely wait for the moment when we would be out of the town where we survived such a horrible air raid. We were passing ruined, burning houses and piled-up railway tracks, next to which lay two dead horses. On the road, there were crowds of refugees, some on bicycles, others on foot or on carts, yet others riding horses bareback. Above the town soared a German plane. The pilot was flaunting his successful mission of destruction and was probably taking photographs of the burning town to show to his "Führer." We were already far away, but he still circled above the town, and there was not a single Polish plane to shoot him down or at least chase him away.

A good way from Siedlce, we suddenly saw two large German bombers flying very low. We jumped out of the car and lay down in the ditch next to the road. The ditch was full of soldiers whom the raid had surprised on the road. They were calm and in control, even though one of the planes passed directly over our heads. At last the planes flew off.

We followed the road leading to Radzyn. Before the town, we stopped at the house of a Jewish horse trader. I can still remember his marvelously beautiful daughter.

In the morning, we continued on our way; several times, we were forced to jump into the ditch because of bombers flying low above ground. One time we hid in a little house. Soon thereafter, we heard shots coming from the nearby cemetery. It turned out that there were soldiers there who were shooting their guns at the airplanes. Needless to say, this World War I method yielded no results and could only contribute to a few bombs being dropped on our heads. Fortunately, it did not come to this, and the two German predators left without leaving any victims on the ground.

Our journey continued through Luboml. We purposefully chose

little-frequented, narrow roads to avoid the air raids on the main thoroughfares. This particular road was terrible, a veritable Sahara. The sand covered the wheels above the axels. It took us several hours to cover a two-kilometer stretch of the road. We actually had to push the car through the sand to make it to Luboml.

Luboml. This was a small, old town, mostly Jewish. The passers-by directed us to the inn. The owner, an old man with a patriarchal beard welcomed us warmly, and soon we felt much at ease there. When I think of Luboml, I can taste the flavor of the wonderful soda water made there. For three grosze, we got a big glass of it that we could barely drink. The water was filling and very tasty. As the following day was the Jewish New Year, there were services in progress at the local synagogue. Suddenly, a German bomber appeared. The drone of its engine created panic among the worshippers. The women were the first to abandon prayers and run into the street. The men followed, deserting the synagogue. Only a few did not interrupt the prayers, and soon they began to call people back to the synagogue. Father returned from the services wishing us a good and sweet year. He told us that he gave to charity on our behalf and that everyone was astounded by his generosity. For dinner, we had chicken soup that, as I noticed, had been cooked in a dirty pot in which the cook had washed her fingers. Halfway through dinner, I found two flies on my spoon and could eat no more. The following day, my sister developed a rash all over her body. I did not know if this could be attributed to the chicken soup or to something else.

Wlodzimierzow. We drove to the next town having covered the car with mud and green branches to mask it from the German pilots' eyes. Still, when we saw the approaching airplanes, we left the car and hid in the bushes by the roadside; unfortunately, those were scarce, as the terrain was sandy and there was hardly any growth. A plane flew down low; had the pilot noticed us? He hadn't; a moment later, he was high up again. We continued on our way while watching the sky with attention because, due to the sound of the car's engine, we could not always hear the droning noise of the German bombers that flew very high.

We were overtaken by several elegant cars flying the British flag. We guessed at once that this must be the staff of the British Embassy, escaping from Warsaw. We caught up with them in Wlodzimierzow; they had the same problem we had with obtaining gas. It was a crisis. We had used up all our reserves, and Father began a search among private people. With great difficulty, we managed to buy several liters at ten zloty a liter, but it was all of different quality. Ten zloty was an exorbitant price at the time and place—an egg in those parts of the country cost three grosze, so that with 10 zloty, one could buy 333 eggs! All this meant that, because of us, small thefts were committed that day: someone stole several liters of gas from a workshop, someone else from a carpenter's. We could not worry about that; we needed gas more than anything else; our lives depended on it.

Kowel. The car was barely moving; every couple of minutes, the carburetor would "shoot"; at last, the engine died. After a moment of consternation, we saved the day by adding a full bottle of pure alcohol to the tank. We stopped the car before entering the town. Four heavy bombers were returning from a raid; we could see the fires. It looked menacing and picturesque all at once. We waited till all was calm and crossed the bridge, which was defended by a lone machine gun. The air raid had not yet been declared over when we entered the town, which was filled with refugees from Lodz and Warsaw. I saw Lodz fire trucks and Warsaw police vehicles there. Under the trees, we saw the bandaged wounded: the victims of the last air raid. A policeman blocked our way out of town.

"The raid is not over," he declared.

Despite my youth, I saw the lack of logic in his argument, and I thought immediately that he wished for the bombs to fall on our heads as well; then he would feel better. Father convinced, him in a few words, of the insubstantiality of his order, and he waved us by. A kilometer farther, we were stopped again; we had to give a ride to a soldier in full uniform. He stood on the step of the seriously overloaded car, and we moved along. His friend tried to stop another car, but in vain; the driver swerved around him expertly.

Luck. We had relatives here, and that is where we stopped. Another air raid. The whizzing of falling bombs began anew. We went down to a very weak cellar and tried to stand under the iron beam. The whizzing approached. A lieutenant who happened to be with us in the cellar suggested that we quickly run to the public shelters, which were nearby. A powerful whiz, and, through the little window above, we saw a red pillar of smoke. I was convinced that a fire had erupted next to us, but it was only the aftermath of the explosion. The siren called off the alarm. The dead and the wounded were carried out of the building and laid in the streets. A great fire near the airport marked that raid as a German victory. Two Polish fighter planes circled above the town—the only two left of the twenty or so that had stood at the airport before the raid. The rest were burned. We were told later by a soldier that the raid took place twenty minutes after the crews left for a lunch break, and that was why the planes were immobile on the field. He was sure that spies had their hand in the outcome of that raid. On the same day, several people were arrested. In their houses were clandestine radio stations. These were apparently important, highly-placed people. We left Luck in a rush, fearing another air raid. First, however, we purchased gas, paying through our noses.

Rowno. We stopped only very briefly, and, of course … there was an air raid. Thinking that we would have to live through another bombing, we looked for a shelter. Mother tripped and fell, wounding her knee. Blood seeped through her stocking. Unexpectedly, without any bombing, the alarm was called off. We immediately returned to the car and moved on, but now without a concrete destination. We looked at the map, but couldn't decide where we should really be going. That was how we passed the river Horyn. On the other side of the bridge was the town of Tuczyn.

Tuczyn. We instinctively headed toward the east. Therefore, we decided to stop here because this was the last little town before the Soviet border. We parked the car in the main square and looked for lodging. It was a poor town, and everyone was eager to offer us accommodation, believing that they could make some money this way. We chose a large house with a big orchard. After having discussed the conditions, the owner allowed us to drive onto the property. The place looked safe if not idyllic, except for the tall chimney of the tannery next door that could attract the enemy pilots' attention. With the help of steel ropes, we managed to lay the chimney flat on the ground. Tuczyn is, to me, the great old apple tree that took up much of the orchard. It was a colossal tree with innumerable golden "pineapple" apples. As the owner let us pick as many as we wished, I spent much of my time under that tree, eating my fill of splendid, juicy, aromatic fruit. Never again did I taste such fruit.

Someone in town had a radio. Warsaw was surrounded, and the heroic speeches of its great president were meant to keep its spirit strong. The front was not a single line; everything was confused. When a certain place was being defended behind the lines, the Germans were already one hundred kilometers farther. The front was, nonetheless, closer and closer to us. Father, a professional optimist, kept saying that the perpetual retreat of the Polish forces was part of the plan of the commander of the Polish Army, General Rydz Smigly. On the other hand, the rumors had it that the Germans were four kilometers away from Luck.

The same night, we were awakened by explosions. We ran onto

the veranda and saw the glow in the west, accompanied by frequent detonations. When, after half an hour, there was no end to this, we began to think that this was no raid, but the front. There was a commotion in the town. Everyone was packing, but they wanted to wait for dawn to have a better understanding of the situation. We too were confused. Sioma thought seriously of going farther east, even if that meant crossing into the Soviet Union. Then everything calmed down and the glow paled. But even though there were no more explosions, we could not sleep that night. In the morning, a formation of Polish planes passed above us.

Father said, "Surely the English have sent their air force, and these are the Polish planes being moved to another front."

After lunch, we saw another plane, high up. It circled around the town, looking a lot like a German plane getting ready to drop bombs. We lay down in the ditch in the garden. When the plane dropped even lower, I barely recognized red stars on its wings, which looked like small dots from the distance. The radio broadcast Molotov's speech. We opened our eyes in amazement; we had thought previously that the Russian Army was arriving to fight the Germans.

Sioma brought the news that the Soviets were already in town. "They arrived in an old car—a wreck from the First World War. They're dirty and poorly dressed."

I wanted to see them badly, so I went to the main square. Trucks were coming, all identical, newly-manufactured; but the model was an old one. Following them was field artillery pulled by horses. All this smacked of dilapidation. The horse-drawn field hospitals must have served already in the war with Japan in 1905. I spent much of the day watching the artillery driving by. When I returned home, everyone was worried by my long absence. Father told me later that when he was in Russia, it happened that the passing army would take children with them by force.

Many of the local Jews greeted the Soviet army with relief. "My uze davno vas zhdali," ("We've been expecting you for a long time,") some said. During the night we heard shots; we thought that they came from the garden next to the house. We lay down on the floor and remained there for several hours. We spent the following night in the house of a merchant on the square because the center of town appeared to be safer. The atmosphere became heavy. People worried more and more about the possibility of an attack on the town by Polish partisans from the surrounding villages. The Poles wanted to take revenge on the Jews who had welcomed the Soviets. All the wooden stakes which made up the fences around the trees on the square were pulled out to serve in self-defense. There were also some Ukrainian peasants in town; they arrived with their own arms—rifles from fifty years earlier—and constituted something of a temporary police force. At night, few people were able to sleep. We heard shots in the distance. Suddenly, floodlights made the square bright. A Soviet truck filled with armed soldiers arrived, greeted by a resounding "Hooray!" and "Now we are afraid no longer."

What was my attitude to the events at hand? Educated in a rather bourgeois school among the children of the greatest snobs in the city, I objected to the welcoming attitude of some local Jews toward the Red Army. I did not know then that one of the factors influencing this partiality was the acute anti-Semitism adopted by the Polish government in the east, even more forcefully than in other parts of the country.

A further stay in Tuczyn did not make sense. We decided to continue on to Luck. It would have been impossible to leave the town by car because the police were confiscating all vehicles, so Sioma dismantled an important part of the engine, and in this way rendered the car non-drivable. We hired horses that pulled the car, where Mother sat with my little sister. We counted on the woman and the child rendering the car untouchable. After five kilometers, a taxi cab caught up with us. A policeman got out with a revolver and a red band on his sleeve. He asked if we had a "rozreshenie" (permit) from the chief of police to take the car out. For a moment, we feared that the car would be lost, but Father, who was following the car on a wagon with me, had an excellent idea. He told the policeman that we were actually in the process of delivering the car to the authorities in Rowno. After a brief conversation with his colleague at the wheel, the policeman waved us along and returned to town.

Rowno. Food was scarce. The stores sold only limited quantities. I remember how I was able to buy eggs twice in the same store. When I already held them in my hand, the saleswoman realized what had happened. I was very uncomfortable, but I controlled myself quickly and told her that we had a very big family to feed. That was enough.

To buy anything, one had to stand in interminable lines. People were eager to spend their money, and they bought up everything. The commander-in-chief of the town was a decent human being. Mother convinced him to issue a permit for the car by explaining that we were transporting a sick child to Wilno.

It was impossible to follow the order making the registration of refugees compulsory. The line to the registration office was several kilometers long. People waited day and night and were hardly any closer because there were only two clerks working, and they were not in a hurry. Father measured with a watch that they used twenty minutes per petitioner, and there were thousands of petitioners. The only solution was to get to the office by a trick. Father and Sioma took a sack of apples and slowly walked to the beginning of the line. When they were by the door, they began offering the apples to the people in line, thus gaining their trust (through the stomach to the heart). When the clerks, who drank tea instead of doing their job were about to close the office, Father and Sioma made it inside and managed to get us registered.

One time, while I was walking in the street, I saw a Polish officer being led by "krasnoarmieytsy" (Red Army soldiers). One Soviet soldier walked in front of the prisoner with his bayonet stuck on the rifle, while the second Soviet followed with the bayonet almost touching the back of the Pole. I felt very sorry for the soldier led in this manner, and I was outraged when I noticed a boy who demonstratively applauded the little convoy from the sides. We left Rowne for Luck in our own car because the pass warranted our safe passage, and gas was available in unlimited quantities for seven rubles a liter.

Luck. We arrived at our relatives' again. They received us rather coolly, but we did not let ourselves be discouraged by this, and we remained in their apartment. They proposed that we stay in the basement, which was not acceptable, so we looked for other lodging. Next door, there was a room for rent in the apartment of a notary who had been arrested by the Soviet authorities. His wife agreed to give us sheets and comforters. We moved there at once and that night slept in clean bedding, feeling like aristocrats.

It was the end of September or beginning of October; the school year was about to begin. There was a large middle school in Luck, and I signed up to attend it. I went there with my cousin Kuba. The level was rather mediocre, much below that of my school in Lodz, so I became at once if not the best, then one of the best students. I could not believe my own progress. The only problem was the foreign language, but only at first. From the first year of my school in Lodz, I hated German, and this was my chance to abandon it, as I had no reports with me, and, anyhow, no one asked for them. When, about a week into the school year, I was asked whether I had studied German or French, I answered without hesitation: English (of which I had a vague notion). That meant I was left in peace as far as foreign languages were concerned, if one doesn't count Latin. Usually, first thing in the morning after we arrived at school, everyone would copy homework from me. Before the war in Lodz, it was the other way around—I copied from others, that is, if my tutor had not already done my homework for me.

What was the frame of mind of the Polish youth and of the society at large at the time? Our Polish teacher appealed to us to be particularly attentive in her class, "as long as they still allow us to study Polish," and she compared our situation to a passage in Stefan Zeromski's *Syzyfowe prace*, even though, to tell the truth, we, the pupils, behaved rather scandalously in class. In the same breath, the teacher also divulged her other complaints about the new authorities, mostly because the teachers had not been paid for three full months, with the excuse that the Polish government had paid them before the war. This was blatantly unfair, as prices had risen to ten times what they had been before the outbreak of the war.

One day, an old convertible stopped in front of the school. Several officers got out and went into the headmaster's office. When they returned twenty minutes later, the roof of the car had been cut out with scissors and was sitting next to the car. The convertible looked funny with torn pieces of canvas hanging on the sides. The whole thing was an overtly hostile act toward the Bolsheviks. The following day, the teachers explained to us that the incident was senseless and could only end badly for the school.

Another time, we were led to a meeting at which a committee was supposed to be elected. A student known to be a communist stood up and read a list of names of fellow students, all of whom were also known for their pro-communist tendencies. They all belonged to the so-called "Godless club." Having read the list of candidates, the leader asked whether anyone was against. I was not sure why, but only one student, a girl, stood up and spoke against this "election." We were almost unanimously on her side, though. Was it the power of suggestion or simple fear that kept us silent? I noticed a similar mechanism at work in all the "elections" that followed; no one objected to the so-called "candidates." The student who did protest left the room all red in the face. I felt great respect for her courage and honorable comportment.

School and homework occupied most of my day. The rest of my time was spent reading the books in our landlady's library. In the first week of our stay in Luck, I had another, very "interesting" entertainment. Not far from our house, there was a former office of the bureau of emigration, now defunct and abandoned. It became the goal of our escapades. Kuba, several other boys, and I would go over there to "rescue" items that were of value to us. Above all, we were interested in the stationery materials. We made off with entire piles of envelopes and office paper. We found this very exciting and would emerge breathless and loaded with goods. Our attention was drawn to some trunks which we could not, however, open. That made them even more tempting, especially since Kuba claimed that there must be typewriters in there. On the very day when we came equipped to break the trunks open, we were chased away by a policeman with a rifle. That was the end of our expeditions in search of the "golden fleece." We undertook them with a clear conscience because everything was derelict so that we, too, felt we had neighborly claims to it.

As our financial situation was not too rosy, Father had to travel to Lwow several times to make some money. He would buy goods there and then sell them in Luck with a 100 percent profit. One time, Father did not return from Lwow at the appointed hour. A day passed, then another, and yet another. Mother simply went mad with worry. She walked in the street and cried; she was so sure that he had been arrested. I kept sending telegrams from the post office. Mother's great anxiety made me extremely anxious as well. When the fourth day went by without my father's return, I told myself that things must be in a bad way indeed. I did not know what to do.

Father arrived on the fifth day. The delay was caused because his passport had been stolen. He had no way of letting us know what had happened because no telegraph was working in Lwow. He arrived and announced immediately that we were leaving for Wilno. As it turned out, Father had heard on the radio that Wilno had been returned to Lithuania, and the Lithuanian army was already in the city. We were supposed to be ready the following morning, and even though my little sister had a fever, we began to pack.

We traveled through the muddy Polesie region. The landscape was typical of Polesie—marshes and bogs—and it continued for many kilometers and was very tedious.

Kobryn. This was our first stop. We were told to hide our car because the Soviet authorities in Kobryn confiscated even the vehicles which had permits. We placed the car by the gate to the inn, but we did not stay there long, and soon we were on our way. We had plenty of gas, enough to get us all the way to Wilno.

The road led through Bialystok, where we had to spend the night. We were too tired to continue driving on without resting the night. One additional reason was a short, but difficult, detour just before the city. I closed my eyes so as not to watch the car become submerged in a bog, and I do not remember how we made it out of there. It so happened that we arrived in Bialystok's poor Jewish district. We found accommodations very quickly and were given plenty of bedding, but I was loath to sleep in it. I preferred to return to the car where Sioma was sleeping. It was bitterly cold outside, and I got chilled to the bone within minutes. There was no way I could fall asleep there, so I returned stealthily to our room, and, despite the unappetizing bedclothes, slept there blissfully. Oh, how well I slept then!

We assumed that the border was not being guarded yet and that we would be able to cross it easily, but just in case, we had a permit issued by the Soviet authorities. To the permit issued for us for Lwow, Wilno had been added. We stuck this permit on the front windshield because, unfortunately, the word "Wilno" was written in a slightly different ink. But through the windshield, everything was a bit blurry, and the ink did not look that off. A soldier lifted his arm to stop us. Yes, this must be the border; I recognized the Russian border guard's cap. "Previerka dokumentov" (document control). Of course, the soldier tore the permit off the windshield and read it; then another soldier arrived, and a third; they all read it, and they shrugged their shoulders. A bad sign. One of them asked why we were leaving the Soviet Union. Father explained that he had relatives in Wilno, that in the car there was a sick child, and that the car with the driver was supposed to return, etc. The soldier's attitude was not aggressive, but knowing the Russian mentality (They can cry with the condemned, but they perform the sentence, nonetheless.), we did not think this boded well. Siomek was already considering trying to cross at a different border point that might not be guarded yet.

At this point, one of the guards began to chat with us. It turned out that the border was guarded as of that day, and he could not, on his own, authorize our passage. If we wished, he could notify "starshina," (an officer) who could then decide himself whether to let us through. We agreed at once, knowing that in the Russian army the higher the rank, the more reasonable the person. The soldier shot in the air three times. This was supposed to be the sign to the "starshina," who was in the neighboring village, that he was needed. We waited. Nobody came. The soldier shot again, but again nobody appeared. He took up his rifle calmly and again three times: *paf, paf, paf.* A car drove up from the Lithuanian border. A Soviet major got out. The soldier made a report. Father, too, walked up to the officer and put forth the sick child as the main motive of our trip. The officer turned out to be a decent man; he let us through without ordering a search of the car. I can imagine the soldiers' disappointment— they had been eyeing our luggage atop the car, thinking that perhaps something would fall to them during that search. We crossed the border with great relief, feeling very happy. We joked, laughed, sang. We passed many refugees who looked at us with envy because we were riding in a car, while they must "per pedes apostolorum" (go by foot) with their belongings on their backs. We were calculating when we would make it to Wilno when a new obstacle blocked our way: a broken bridge. A rather wide river flowed calmly below. There was no other way across it, and it was impossible to drive through the river, which was too deep.

"We're not going to wait for them to build a new bridge, are we?" the men fussed. Luckily, there was a village nearby. Several local people gathered around the car. They claimed it would be possible to go across in the car. We drove in slowly. I was sure that the engine would be flooded, but no, it was not. The water, however, did flood the interior of the car. Now it seemed that nothing would interrupt our progress toward Wilno.

We passed the first Lithuanian patrols on their way to the border. The Lithuanians struck us as very tall and strong: "boys like oak trees." On a house in one of the villages, we saw the Lithuanian flag. What a strange feeling. We were in Lithuania.

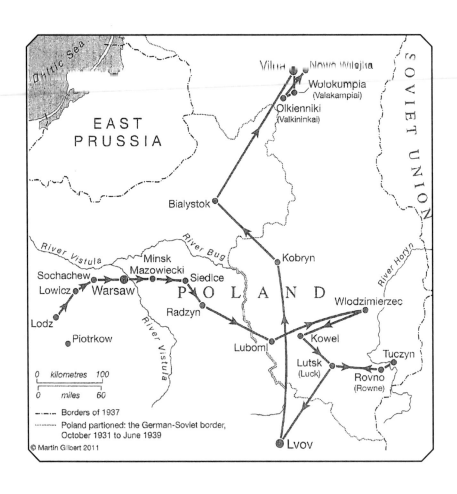

CHAPTER TWO

WE APPROACHED THE CITY quickly; its lights were already visible. In a couple of minutes, we were at the city gates. We crossed the suburbs. The Lithuanian policemen, at least six feet tall, were in the streets in operetta outfits (like imperial Hungarian soldiers). Their tall, cylinder-like hats added to their stature. We laughed at these outfits and at their tall owners. We arrived at the house of my father's uncle, where they told us they had been expecting us for several days already. They welcomed us with a dinner, which to me had an exquisite taste because it had been long since I had such delicacies as, for instance, cheese, a whole chunk of which lay on a plate, tempting us. There were also other dainties, and then there was a good night's sleep on a fine bed and with a calm heart. I thought I was in paradise.

But, the same night, I went to town with Sioma. There were crowds of people in the streets, many of them refugees. The Lithuanian army was riding all over town, singing songs. A strange atmosphere hung in the air—almost an air of relaxation. On the second day, we moved to another place so as not to depend on our relatives, who, we felt, were not too enthusiastic about our staying with them. We moved to my father's aunt's home, but we promised to pay rent, which in any case was a blessing for the aunt, who had no source of income as her husband was in Warsaw.

Again, we had no luck with people. The aunt, in her looks, resembled a witch. Her foremost vice, avarice, was clear to me in a matter of minutes, when I saw that, as she took off the lampshade, she counted the pins that held it together. This aunt had a servant and a confidant: the hunchbacked Nastja. Both women looked like heroines of a novel. An additional element of the atmosphere was a cat, Murichka, present daily in the apartment. The place was permeated with that peculiar odor of old age, and it was most concentrated in the aunt's room. In the kitchen, that odor mixed with another, highly unpleasant, smell that I thought to be the smell of Nastja the servant. Two very old people— together they counted 160 years at least—lived in one of the rooms. They never aired it out, so when I once entered their room by accident, I almost threw up.

The house was in a peaceful and pretty neighborhood on Wielka Pohulanka Street. There was a large park nearby, where we often went for walks later. It was very cold when we arrived in Wilno. Even though we had brought a lot of things with us, we did not have a full wardrobe for each family member, and so I had to survive November chills in a light overcoat.

Soon, I began to attend the Epsztajn Middle School. I remember my first day at the school. Upon entering the classroom, I sat down next to a pleasant girl. There were more girls than boys in the class, so at once they began to whisper to each other on my account. The teacher was helpless, and his attempts to quiet the class down had no effect. Pedagogically speaking, the class was lost. I was rather proud that my person had caused such commotion. Then I saw an expression of surprise on the faces. It disappeared after I answered the first few questions I was asked. As it turned out, they had taken me for a Pole who came to the school by mistake; the school was 100 percent Jewish. Further questioning about my origins caused much contentment among a group of boys who themselves were "biezentsy"—refugees. Many natives of Wilno treated "biezentsy" with compassion mixed with contempt, granted to those whose only property were the clothes they had on their backs. I befriended one of the "biezentsy," Tadek

Wajdenfeld. Quite miraculously, Tadek and his parents survived the war, and he is now one of my closest friends.

The Epsztajn Middle School was very pleasant. I liked the fact that the distance between the teacher and the pupils was underplayed. Our professors did not spare us bad grades, but they did this in a friendly manner, unlike their counterparts in Lodz who were very formal. After my first failing grade, I began to study with great fervor. I learned thoroughly and systematically, and thus I soon became one of the top five students and remained there for the remainder of my time at the school. And to think that, before the war, being a good student seemed beyond my reach! I had not even attempted to be good. Instead, despite all the tutoring, I had had the distinction of being in the bottom five of my class.

My tutors were graduates of the same school and, by then, good friends of the teachers who dealt us the Fs. The only class that posed some difficulty at Epsztajn was the Lithuanian language. I failed the final exam, which meant that I had to take it again after the summer. In order to pass it, I had to study hard with the help of a poor Jewish tutor. He had a stomach ruined by dining in cheap eating-houses, and his indigestion usually took up one-third of each class.

The school year passed very quickly. I prepared furiously for the exams, which, if I passed, would grant me the "small matura" (pre-final graduation exam). I had a ton of work, but the material was well organized, so I ploughed through it with ease. The exams—except for the Lithuanian language—went well, and I felt that I practically had the diploma in my hand. I could enjoy the world, especially since I had no other troubles. Father was providing for us handsomely, and we were all in good health. I even began to earn a bit of my own money by giving dance lessons to my classmates. Before the war, my parents had sent me to a dance school where I learned the English waltz, the foxtrot, the slow fox, and the tango. For music, I used an old gramophone with a winding-key and several dusty, cracked records. I remember one of the songs was "Gorace bubliczki," (hot bagels), sung in Russian, probably from the times of Tsar Nicholas I. I do not remember how much I charged per lesson, but I collected the money after each lesson and felt very rich indeed.

The rest of our family was in Warsaw, and we were in contact with them by mail. We sent them numerous packages with food, and we wired them money. We also attempted to bring them to Wilno. We sent someone for Mother's sister with her little girl and for Father's mother, but this did not work out. They were caught at the border and sent back. The second attempt to bring them to Wilno was also fruitless and quite nerve wracking. We received news that the Germans had caught them and that they were in prison. Mother was mad with worry and could think of nothing else but how to save them. "We'll send money to a lawyer who will defend them in court." (This was before we knew what the Germans were all about.)

To have a clear picture of the situation, the men went to the border and obtained information there. They learned that the crossing of the border was indeed unsuccessful, but that our relatives had not been arrested. As if to confirm this, we received a telegram from Warsaw telling us that they were in one piece and well, back in Warsaw. We breathed with relief. That was our last attempt to get them out; further attempts were technically impossible. The Warsaw ghetto was taking shape. The family wrote from there that an official order to set up the ghetto had been given. Since they were living on Swietojerska Street, they did not have to move, which was considered good fortune. Full of misgivings, we begged them not to let themselves be locked up in the ghetto and to escape from Warsaw. We believed that, in the provinces, they would have an easier time finding food than in the walled-in ghetto.

A few weeks before the final closing of the ghetto, Aunt Rysia let us know indirectly that there was a possibility of a fictitious conversion to Christianity and that was a way to leave the ghetto. These hints were repeated several times in the letters, until finally they wrote that they were "Walled in." They were at the mercy of an enemy whose cruelty they ignored almost completely. We were in despair. Subconsciously, we knew that their lives were in danger. But the contact through the mail did not stop, and we continued to send packages with food and money. One day, they received three packages at once, and they wrote afterward that we should not send that much because they feared unpleasant consequences of having a large stash. Aunt Rysia began to attend sewing classes that would last three years. The poor thing did not know that she would not even complete half of the course. The letters started to come more and more rarely, and they bore the stamp "Judenrat Warschau."

Our financial situation was still excellent. Father, who knew a lot about diamonds, began to trade in them, at first as a middleman. He then bought them on his own and sold them at a good profit. There was a great demand for diamonds. Father sold them mostly in Kowno, where they were bought up by embassy and consulate employees. That is why there was a significant difference in price between Wilno and Kowno, and it was profitable to buy them in Wilno.

My father's encounter with Count Plater-Zyberk opened new possibilities. The majority of Polish landed gentry from Eastern Poland resided in Wilno as refugees. Deprived of their estates and hence of their income, they were supporting themselves by selling their valuables. Mr. Plater, as a Polish aristocrat, spent a lot of time among the gentry and served as a middleman between them and Father for a handsome commission. There were days when Father and Jan Plater made hundreds of lits (Lithuanian currency). We were quite shocked, therefore, when we learned of the planned merger of Lithuania with the Soviet Union. Like many other refugees, Father attempted to obtain permission to go abroad. In those times, Polish intelligentsia gathered mainly at the Intelligentsia Club on Wielka Pohulanka Street next to Zawalna. The place was spacious, well lit, and warm, so I went there often to meet friends from Warsaw, boys with whom I had attended the Epsztajn Middle School. Another person whom I would find there was Miss Irka, an attractive young woman I had befriended.

At home, we also had a young lady, my little sister's tutor, the twenty-nine-year-old Miss Janina, who quickly earned our respect through her refinement and her devotion to our family. She had studied natural sciences, and nature was her favorite subject, which she discussed whether it was appropriate or not. She liked animals, told stories about them, and showed us pictures of herself riding a horse. She boasted about her horseback riding exploits and talked about horses much of the time. Now and then, she would arrange games in which I had to search for an object hidden by her on her person, which gave me the excuse to stroke her beautiful breasts. She did not begrudge me that in the least. I was sixteen years old by then and more and more often had immodest thoughts. Soon, however, Miss Janina had to leave us to accept more advantageous employment at an estate. She was supporting her mother and did not earn enough at our house for both of them. We parted with her with true regret because we could feel her genuine attachment to our family and goodness of character. Much later, at a moment critically important to us, she came to visit us and offered her help. Her successor, Miss Pilsudska, a distant relative of Marshall Pilsudski, disgusted me beyond words, and I avoided her like the plague.

I spent the 1940 summer vacation partly in Wilno and partly in a nearby resort called Wolokumpia. The place was in the woods by the river, so those last carefree vacations were made pleasant by frequent boat excursions. We stayed in a pension owned by the sister of our neighbor on Wielka Pohulanka Street. I would like to say a few words about those neighbors, the Orluk family. They lived one floor below us. We met them because they had a radio, with which all of us listened to news from the front. The Orluks had a sixteen-year-old daughter, who was of average beauty but well-developed physically. Once, when she was alone in the apartment, I went down to see her under some pretext, and I told her that "because I'm very honest, I will say why I came: to fondle you." She only smiled in reply. Afterward, we often went to the movies together.

Mrs. Orluk's family was numerous in Wilno. Her parents, Mr. and Mrs. Kotlar, lived with their youngest daughter, Ida, at 17 Weglowa Street. Another daughter lived in Olkienniki, while the daughter who owned the pension in Wolokumpia where we were staying lived by herself in Wilno. She was a widow. My mother's brother Sioma enjoyed flirting with the youngest one, Ida.

After the entry of Soviet troops into Wilno, we moved out of the apartment on Pohulanka Street. Many circumstances contributed to this decision, but the chief reasons were our aunt's continued intrigues and the rumors she spread about us. She would pass on fantastic news about us to any family member who would listen. In addition, we would hear from acquaintances that she "supported us." Our firewood would disappear regularly, stolen by the aunt and her other tenants. In those days, firewood was extremely expensive. We bought it in bundles, but it disappeared in front of our very eyes, and we could never buy enough. At first, we thought that the stoves were simply very inefficient, but then we concluded otherwise. This, however, had to be proven. I verified that the wood was indeed being stolen by arranging it in a particular manner and then finding it disturbed upon our return home. Something had to be done.

I inconspicuously marked each log with ink. I knew when the tenants would fire the stove, and I left the house fifteen minutes before then. When I surreptitiously returned, the wood was already aflame in the stove. I opened the stove door. Identical logs would not have been able to tell their story, but my markings on them confirmed the theft. Among the not-yet-burned logs were some that belonged to us. I could not stand my aunt, who by mere appearance resembled the Baba Yaga, and neither did I like her tenants for the offensive stench that emanated from their apartment. That is why I decided to punish them with a scene. I immediately poured water over the logs. One of the tenants, who had already noticed my mysterious manipulations near the stove, came out of her room and began to lament loudly, but I shouted louder yet. All the members of the household ran to the corridor where I stood, all proud that I had caught the "criminals" who had been contributing to our extraordinary expenses in times that were not so extraordinarily prosperous any longer. As "corpus delicti," I showed all those interested the ink marks on the half-burned logs, pulled out of the stove.

Father announced that he'd had enough of my aunt's hospitality and would look at once for another place to live. Soon we moved to an apartment on Zawalna Street, where, up to then, the two uncles had lived on their own: Sioma and Mietek, aunt Rysia's husband. (Aunt Rysia was my mother's sister.) Uncle Mietek had left Lodz on foot soon after our departure, and, with great difficulty, he had managed to arrive in Wilno.

When the Epsztajn Middle School changed the language of instruction to Yiddish—a language I did not speak—I had to transfer to Adam Mickiewicz Middle School, later renamed the State Middle School Number 3, where all subjects were taught in Polish. I attended the ninth grade, where the foreign language was English, taught by a dry, bony lady who enjoyed giving Fs. The homeroom teacher was Mr. Baltrukiewicz, famous both within and without the school for his sayings. For example, he was known to address students as follows: "You good-for-nothing, that in Wilno we call *zhulik*, and in French *apache*, tell me now …" He did not say such things in anger; on the contrary, his attitude was quite paternal, and students adored him. The short and bald chemistry teacher, on the other hand, was our victim. We behaved horrendously in his class, often forcing him to abandon the classroom. He lectured very ineptly, and few among us could boast a passing grade in chemistry. One thing we knew by heart was the structure of a water molecule, H_2O, because he spent at least a month on that. Otherwise, we knew next to nothing. Mr. Kowalski, our physics teacher, explained everything in great detail and very clearly. I liked him a lot, and I was, perhaps, the best student in his class. Thus I knew physics best, as well as mathematics and trigonometry. Our Polish teacher was an interesting type. He was very progressive and taught us liberalism, tolerance, and socialism. Most boring of all were the lectures on Stalin's constitution, "the wisest of all constitutions in the world," in the words of our lecturer. History, even though taught by the same teacher, was, nonetheless, very interesting, even with his communist bias. I was a good student, even though expectations were high and opportunities to slack abounded. Since we were the junior class, we were collecting the names of the voters before the elections to the "soviets." This lasted almost a month, which we spent very merrily, doing little electoral work while we traveled widely in free buses. Nearly once a week, we had to attend propaganda meetings. As long as the speaker was intelligent, time passed quickly. My contemporary change of mentality can perhaps be attributed to the influence of these meetings. The way I looked at the world and its problems began to change, and the communist world appeared to me to be the ideal. I attended the meetings more and more willingly, and I applauded their concluding statements more and more ardently. Later, however, my views changed completely as I observed the division into classes in the Soviet system: the exact opposite of the ideal communist society whose superiority I upheld at the time.

My father continued to do well financially. He continued to buy and sell diamonds. We sent huge sums of money to Warsaw via unofficial channels, so-called "transfers." We also accumulated a lot of jewelry and gold objects which, together with our pre-war possessions, represented a great value. In preparation for our departure abroad, the three most precious pieces of jewelry, namely pearls, a sapphire-and-ruby studded butterfly, and sapphire earrings, were hidden in a hand mirror and in a wooden bootjack. Later on, in Horodyszcze, I buried and dug up the bootjack many a time in the garden next to the house. Just before the evacuation of the town, I could not find it. I dug in several directions, until at last I found the precious bootjack with its load. The butterfly brooch survived the war, and it has its place in my testament—it will be able to rest and tell its story. The remaining pieces of jewelry were in a bureau drawer. Afraid of all the possible scenarios, my mother and I insisted on hiding those things as well, to which Father invariably answered, "This is mine, and no one has the right to take it from me."

We feared more and more the consequences of the trade my father carried on so nonchalantly; he was not very discreet about it, and in town was known as the "diamond king," which in Soviet times meant "igranie z ogniom" (playing with fire). When I sometimes consider the fact that, despite the fame that surrounded my father as the "diamond dealer," the NKVD left us alone until May 1941 (one month before the German invasion), I can attribute it either to our extraordinary good luck or to the extraordinary inaptitude of their informers.

My uncle Mietek Chigryn carried on a different kind of trade. His specialties were headache powder (which later on turned out to be mustard), hard currency, and even cocaine. Once, he burst into our apartment pale in the face and announced that someone had taken from him the five hundred dollars that Father had given him to sell. Father absorbed half of the loss. Later, we learned that the money was taken by a man to whom Mietek had sold bad cocaine or even an ersatz. Mietek's business partner in most of these transactions was Mrs. Paprocka, an engineer's wife, the same person who traveled in vain to Warsaw to get our relatives.

My father's later arrest and his forced departure to a distant part of Russia were also connected with this woman. One day, Mr. Lisawoder, an acquaintance of my father's from Lwow, arrived with another man. He brought with him an ingot of gold worth thousands of rubles. Father was supposed to sell it, and as Mrs. Paprocka told Mietek she knew someone who was interested in it, that was where the gold was taken. Father and Mietek were already counting their profits. Mrs. Paprocka, however, returned the gold, and, to all appearances, the transaction had been canceled. The following day, a man came with two thousand rubles as a deposit and a message from Mrs. Paprocka that there was another potential buyer and that Father should take the gold to her house, which he did. They agreed that the money would be delivered a few hours later. Mr. Lisawoder, his partner, Father, and Mietek Chigryn were all at our place waiting for the rest of the money. They were calm because the gold was in trusted hands. Father, Mr. Lisawoder, and his partner were sitting at a table chatting, while Mietek, fully dressed, was lying on the bed, and I was sitting next to him. I wasn't feeling particularly well; I had a headache and was coming down with the flu.

The doorbell that rang at that moment was identical to ringing doorbells that resounded in our apartment daily, and yet it announced the arrival of people very different from those who usually visited us. That doorbell announced the beginning of a tragic period in the life of our family. Even though September 1939 was not exactly an easy period, and the year and a half we spent in Wilno could not be compared to our normal pre-war life in Lodz, nonetheless, the period that was beginning was such that it made us remember with nostalgia the bombs falling on Siedlce.

Three of them entered the apartment: a Russian, a Jew, and a Lithuanian. While the Russian and the Lithuanian came only as far as the dining room, the Jew "marched" into the bedroom. I didn't understand what this was all about and who these people were. Only later, when the Russian demanded to see our documents and showed us his ID, did everything become clear. I thought that they were off the mark since, at that moment, we had neither the ingot of gold nor any hard currency at home, and the jewelry and the gold watches were our personal property "that no one can take away from us," as Father kept saying, all the more since these things were not hidden, but were in an old chocolate box in the bureau drawer. That alone should show that they were "kosher"; otherwise they would be hidden away, I thought.

The agent who had gone into the bedroom began the search. He started with the desk and, naturally, happened upon the chocolate box right away. Wearing a triumphant expression, he came into the room where his colleagues were busy searching, and he put the jewelry on the table, next to the thick folds of banknotes found on the hapless merchants from Lwow. When he was done with the desk, he opened the wardrobe and began to finger the lining of the suits and other clothes hanging there. In the lining of one of the ladies' jackets, there were ordinary lead weights (so it would fit well). They were oval and on touch could resemble coins. The sleuth who discovered these weights was already convinced that he had found gold dollars. He smiled, his eyes lit up, and he began slashing the lining of the jacket with a razor blade he had taken out of his pocket. Soon he pulled out the "dollars" sewn into fabric and, having reached the "core," saw that, instead of the glitter of gold, there was only lead. Even then he did not give up at once. He bent the piece of lead and only threw it away after having examined it carefully. He repeated this procedure with yet another piece of "gold" and at last abandoned the search.

In the end, the search was short and superficial. It seemed that the agents had received instructions as to where to look for things, or that, having happened upon exposed jewelry, they did not expect to find anything else in our house. They did not even touch the furniture and things on the second floor. Mietek Chigryn still lay on the bed, fearing for his own skin as well as for the leather hidden behind the wardrobe. There were some small gold objects in the suitcases up on the wardrobe, and those remained untouched as well.

The Russian, who was the most genteel of the three men, wrote down a report. And there was a lot to write down: the table was covered with jewelry and gold watches, including Grandfather Leon's watch. The most striking piece of all was Mother's four-carat diamond ring. Most of these things had come with us from Lodz. We had no idea that we wouldn't see them again, convinced that when the authorities realize that those were our private possessions and not objects for trade, they would return them. Father even obtained the address where he should attempt to reclaim them. The process of documenting the search took a long time because each object was described in detail.

When the Russian finished filling the page with his indelible pencil, he signed it and handed it over to us for signature. Then he wrapped the fruit of the search in several newspapers and said something to the Lithuanian, who immediately went downstairs. By some strange quirk of fate, more people came to see us that day than ordinarily, and we were worried that one of these visitors might bring a compromising "load." Each arriving visitor was searched thoroughly. One poor lady had her glasses case and her shoes searched. Fortunately, they all had come to see us on private matters, and none carried anything forbidden. No one was let out of the apartment, so in the end there were over a dozen people inside: the "persecutors," the "victims," and the "innocents." The room was stuffy and filled with cigarette smoke. I was almost sick to my stomach; my nerves at first taut with the tension of watching strangers rummaging through our personal things now gave in, and I felt indifferent to everything. My ears were buzzing.

When the Lithuanian came back, we understood that he had gone to telephone for the prison van. My father and the two partners from Lwow were told to get dressed and go downstairs. The following day, Mother took a basket filled with food and drink to the prison, where the guards refused to take it. "My samy ich snabzajem" ("We take care of them ourselves."), they said.

Money was tight. We had to live more frugally. Taking advantage of Father's arrest, one of the middlemen, named Dmowski, did not return the things that Father had given him to sell. Another middleman followed suit. Mother kept traveling from Kovno to Wilno, trying in vain to obtain Father's release through so-called "machers" (persons, who using money, were sometimes able to influence the authorities). For the first few days after Father's arrest, life at home was havoc. Meals were not prepared on time, the apartment was neglected, and so forth. Then we got used to Father's absence, and normal life resumed. At about that time, we got news that Mrs. Paprocka had collaborated with the NKVD, and, since neither she nor Chigryn, with whom she was involved in various shady affairs, was arrested, we realized that she must have had something to do with Father's arrest. Needless to say, we never again had news of the ingot of gold she had had.

June, the month of final exams at school, began. In the midst of intense intellectual effort, I tried not to think of what had befallen us, and I passed all the exams. The summer was hot. There was no question of leaving for a vacation, but we did send my little sister to Olkienniki, where she could enjoy fresh air and freedom instead of the tension-filled life at Zawalna Street.

On one of those June days, Mother, as she always did in the morning, went grocery shopping. We noticed that traffic was unusually busy that day. Earlier, we had heard of supposed deportations, but we did not believe these were true. It seemed too horrible to be real. Nonetheless, logic suggested that if there had been deportations in Lwow and other cities, then they were also possible in Wilno. I was still in bed when

Mother went to the market. Mietek, who at the time was employed as a manager at the airport, had left very early. Sioma had been managing a large auto repair garage in Kovno for about six months, so I was home all by myself. The doorbell rang. I jumped out of bed to get the door. *Who could it be, so early?* I asked myself, surprised. Mother had just left, so it couldn't be her, returning with the groceries. I opened the door gingerly.

"Why, it's you!" I said, seeing Mother, pale in the face and without any groceries. "Quickly, get dressed! They're deporting people! I saw a truck in which armed soldiers were guarding people. It's awful. They can be here any minute." Half a minute later I was dressed. We locked the rooms and ran out in the street. We went to Weglowa 17, to the Kotlars'. We thought we would be safer there; they could come to look for us in the apartment, since Father had been arrested, but what could they want from the Kotlars? On the way, we saw trucks filled with people, things, and soldiers with bayonets. At the Kotlars, everyone was in a panic as well. No one was sure who would be deported. No house was spared at least one deportation. From a distance, I saw precisely such an "action": an old woman and her two daughters were "invited" to a car. Both daughters carried bundles; the mother was empty-handed.

At noon, the traffic calmed down. We worried about our things left in the apartment and also wanted to ask the janitor whether "they" had come to get us. We walked slowly toward our apartment, feigning calm while everything was boiling on the inside, as if we were being chased. We ran into the janitor in front of the house; she was not sure whether she herself would be deported. Her things were packed. We asked if they had come for us.

"No one's come, but they could come any moment," she told us.

Despite that, we decided to go upstairs. When cars stopped nearby and the doors shut with a characteristic sound, we held our breath. We moved all our things into one room and then locked it. With a small suitcase containing the most indispensable items and the jewelry in the bootjack and the mirror frame, we returned to Weglowa 17. There, we found Sioma, who had come from Kowno, worried about us. Again, the endless traffic resumed; we heard the cars stopping next door. Just in case, we all hid in the garden. The only people left in the house were the Lithuanians, who, if they came to get them, were ready to go without resistance.

Now and then, the doorbell alarmed us, causing us to nestle down in the bushes so as not to be seen. We acted like ostriches, burying our heads in the sand: only the most foolish optimism could make us believe that they wouldn't search the garden if they came for us. In fact, the bell that shook our nerves every couple of minutes announced friends who, afraid to stay at home, came to us in search of asylum. We spent the night in our clothes, without sleeping a wink. The characteristic sound of slammed car doors, the nerve-wracking promise of an "excursion" to Kazakhstan, were even more audible at night. The following day, we changed our tactics. We walked the streets all day. Since they were not taking people from the streets, we thought it must be safer to be in the street than at home.

We stopped by the apartment. It was already noon. A stranger brought a cigarette packet with a few words written on it. He said that it was a message from someone who had been taken away from our apartment. We thought that it was a mistake. No one had been taken away from our apartment. I looked at the cigarette packet: "train number … car number …" The rest is illegible.

"A mistake," my mother and I confirmed, and we went out once more. We felt safer in the town. But we saw a number of scenes in which entire families were being taken away. A truck standing on Wielka Pochulanka Street was stuffed full of things: trunks and bundles of sheets. A Jewish family was being taken away. Among the people, I recognized a friend from school, a boy slightly older than me. Then we ran into Nastja, my aunt's servant girl. She was very kind and, understanding the situation herself, she offered us a place to sleep in her current employer's house.

We took advantage of her offer eagerly. It was dark when we entered the apartment on Wielka Pochulanka that we knew so well. In the small servant's room, we felt safer than in our apartment on

Weglowa Street, and the night spent on the floor passed much faster than the previous night. At dawn, we left as quietly as we came in. Nastja refused to take the twenty rubles my mother tried to give her for the night and told us we could come back again if we needed to. This is when I remembered that we had heard of people asking as much as one hundred rubles to put up a single person for one night, claiming they should be compensated for taking such a risk.

We returned home, where everything seemed to be in order. No one had come to get us. This calmed us a bit, especially since there was also less car traffic, which led us to believe that the deportations had stopped. Miss Janinka came by to see us. She said that she had packed all the important things that could be carried, above all mattresses because "there is no telling whether there will be something to sleep on where they take us, and good sleep is essential." Each member of her family had a light mattress rolled up to take with them.

Around noon, a man came by with a message and a piece of paper. What he told us was so strange and incomprehensible, so unexpected that it appeared impossible. We did not know what to think. My mother's nerves snapped. "They took him away! They took him! We'll never see him again! Woe is me!"

Now we understood that the message given to us the day before was from my father, so it was conceivable that he was already on the way from Nowa Wilejka, the train station from which the trains carrying the deported were leaving. We decided to see with our own eyes where matters stood. We conquered the pain and began to act. My mother went to buy food, while I began to pack pillows, blankets, and sheets to take to my father. Miss Janinka helped me. When my mother returned, we put the food into a leather bag from a travel service because we had no other bag handy. We added a few bottles of tea and left for Nowa Wilenka.

I do not remember how and by what means we got there, but I remember clearly the sight that awaited us. Long trains stood on the tracks, each car with small barred windows, behind which there were faces of men, women, and children. On the side of each car, a wooden gutter protruded; next to these were pools of excrement and urine. It stank unbearably everywhere; it was a torrid day. Two people in white smocks poured some kind of liquid onto the sewage in front of the cars. From two cars that stood apart came the sound of children crying. In another car, a woman was having a heart attack; someone was screaming, "Doctor! Doctor!" The Red Army soldier on guard walked up to the hospital car to look for a doctor who was not there. A young woman who was in the same car with the woman suffering the heart attack said to her friend, who stood outside the car, "It is so terrible here, so hot, there is no air. One woman is dying already. My brother is the only man in this car. You understand how horrible this is."

With a sack on my back and the bag in my hand, I looked for the train with my father. My mother and I spent half an hour going around, very begrudgingly allowed to pass by the NKVD guards. The sack was mercilessly heavy, but I did not rest even for a moment. At last, a woman we met gave us the information, and we reached the train we were looking for. Passing by each car, we called out, "DAWID DYNIN, DAWID DYNIN." Finally, toward the end of the trains, someone shouted, "He's here. He's here." We saw my father in the wide opening between the doors of the car. His face was yellow, and he was emaciated. He was overjoyed to see us, asking above all for something to drink. The prisoners threw us a piece of string through the window of the car, and we attached the bag with food and drink to the string. Once it was unloaded, they lowered it back down to me. Then the NKVD guard opened the door a little more, and I pushed in the sack with the other things in it. I was immediately relieved to be rid of the sack and to know that I had delivered it to my father.

My father told us that the Germans had given the Soviet Union a forty-eight-hour ultimatum and that the war was sure to start very soon. I was so very tired that I received the news with indifference. *Let whatever comes, come,* I thought, and I promptly forgot everything my father said. My mother returned to town to try to obtain my father's release, while I remained at the station. Soon thereafter, a group of Red Army soldiers walked over to the car and chased me away. I hid behind the trains standing on the next track, and from there, I watched all that was happening in front of my father's car. They read everybody's name from a list and then led them away. My only goal was not to lose sight of them: the prisoners and the soldiers. I was afraid that I'd never be able to find my father again amid the thousands of cars. I crawled underneath cars to avoid the guards. At last they stopped in front of a car and ordered the prisoners to go in. When the soldiers left, I approached the car. My father and the other prisoners were amazed by how quickly I had found them. Almost everyone handed me a piece of paper with addresses of their relatives so that I could inform them about their fate. As I wanted to try to help my mother in her efforts to free my father, I said good-bye to my father and his fellow prisoners and left. I had no certainty that I would ever see my father again, and I swallowed tears bravely during our farewell.

When I got home, it was already six o'clock. My mother and I went to see one of the main officers of the NKVD (national police) because we had heard that, thanks to him, one of our friends destined for deportation had been freed. He was not home, but his wife, a pretty young woman, asked us to sit down and wait for him. He arrived shortly, a tall broad-shouldered man, "W czom dzielo?" (What is this about?) he asked. My mother explained that my father had been taken away from prison to be deported, but that he was innocent, and she asked him to intervene on father's behalf. The officer listened to the explanation and promised to review the file. That was the end of our visit. We were supposed to come the following day to get an answer.

After the visit, I started at once to deliver the various little letters and notes given to me by the prisoners. I walked all over the town because the addresses were from all over. Some families were already informed. Unfortunately, some of the addresses were not accurate. I spent a lot of time trying, sometimes in vain, to locate the families whose addresses were inexact. It got late. The streets were empty. The deportations had ceased. I still had a fair number of notes to deliver and decided that I'd do it the following day. At home, I found my mother, who had been waiting for me anxiously. We thought it best to spend the night at Nastja's, and so that was where we went. We passed a good night; there were no more deportations for the time being. I got up before dawn to finish delivering the messages. In one of the notes, there was the request to give the bearer one hundred rubles and a … spoon. It was a note from a son to his elderly father who lived by himself. The father gave me a spoon with the initials J.W. (Jerzy Walicki) and the requested hundred rubles, but I was not allowed to hand the prisoner the spoon, as it was made of metal. I never had the opportunity to return it, and we used it throughout the war. When it got lost during the return trip to Lodz, I was quite saddened because that object had accompanied us through the worst moments of our lives, and I treated it as a meaningful memento.

At last, I finished the deliveries, which I had done in haste. I was practically running all over town in my loose breeches, which were at the point of falling down, as I had lost a lot of weight. With my wind-blown head of hair, loose breeches, and an exhausted expression, I must have been quite a sight; all the passers-by stared at me. When I got home, a bag with food and drink for my father was already waiting. Without losing a second, I went directly to the bus station and from there on to Nowa Wilejka. It was late morning when I entered the area of the railroad depot. On my way, I ran into group of relatives of the people who were in the same train with my father. "If you are looking for the Wilno train, you have come too late; they have been taken away," somebody told me. They were so convinced that the train had left that they did not even listen when I suggested that we look for it, nonetheless. They told me that the railroad workers confirmed that that particular set of train cars had already left for Moldyczew. I went on looking, driven by a powerful conviction that the train was still there. I felt as if I must fulfill a most important mission: to find the prisoners, to deliver the greetings from their families, to give my father the provisions. My task was to find them among the hundreds of railroad tracks. First, I walked to where the cars stood the day before—in vain. Now and then a train left the station. There were moments when I believed that the train with my father in it had indeed left already.

The other part of the depot extended near a tall hill, from which one could see the long lines of trains. I climbed the hill and looked for the numbers of the trains standing the closest to me. I could only see those, as the numbers of the other trains were not visible. I could only see the faces of the people in the cars. Suddenly, I heard a voice shouting in the distance, once and again. I noticed a hand waving to me from a train standing on the second track from the hill. "It's here!" I heard someone call. Those were my father's fellow travelers, who recognized me from far away. The entire car rejoiced at my arrival. I was the only person who had made it to them that day from town. Without further delay, they pulled up and unloaded the bag with food. Father asked what Mother was doing. I recounted our attempts to obtain his release, which cheered him up.

The air was heavy with June heat. I was parched and could only imagine how thirsty the prisoners must have been. There was no water in the vicinity, so I had to return all the way to the station building to get them some tea. The woman at the refreshment counter refused to accept money for the tea when I told her for whom I was getting it. This stood in dramatic contrast to the attitude of the peasant women I passed on my way to the station. They carried dozens of milk cans, but refused to sell me milk, explaining that the prisoners in the cars would give them a better price. I also bought, with all the money I had on me, bottles of lemonade, and then delivered all the drinks to the car. The guards did not object; only one older military policeman opened the bottles of lemonade, one by one, to make sure that none of them contained alcohol.

I spent the remaining time in conversation with Father. He wanted to know if any of the people to whom he had given jewelry to sell before his arrest had brought it back to us. There was only one man, Dmowski, who had not returned a large diamond and a gold bracelet. That meant a lot of money we could have used, since we had no income and many unpredictable expenses connected to my father's deportation. We gave Father fifteen hundred rubles for the road, leaving less than that for ourselves. Father talked about unavoidable war with the Germans.

It was clear that he expected that war to bring him freedom because he spoke about it with joy, rather than with sorrow. As for me, I was too upset to think about the future, that is, about the war and its consequences. I promised Father that I would come once more after lunch and set out for home. There, my mother told me about her return visit to the NKVD officer in command. His reply was brief: "Wasz muz prestupnik." (Your husband is a criminal.)

When I returned to the station after lunch, there were fewer trains there than earlier. Approaching the track on which my father's car had stood that morning, I saw the departing train. It was the train carrying my father toward the unknown.

The next day passed without thoughts and without hope. Resigned, we stopped trembling out of fear that we'd be taken away. Mother kept repeating that, if not for us—the children—she would have left with Father. Our radio was in a repair shop being fixed, so for the time being we had no news. We thought that the lull in deportations was temporary and that they would resume soon. After all, we saw more cattle cars standing ready at the station. We were unspeakably tired.

Sunday at dawn, we were surprised by an air raid alert. *Are these exercises or war?* we asked ourselves. Soon, the distant sound of bombings convinced us that this was war. We went down to the cellar without haste; we were not afraid of bombs. At the time, it seemed to us that nothing could be worse than deportations, which affected us deeply. The air raid was called off, but a few moments later, it resumed. Again, we went downstairs. This time we could hear the buzzing of many airplanes over the city. Bombs started to fall, closer and closer and louder and louder and … We heard the whistle right above our heads. We nestled up to the wall and closed our eyes. A tremendous bang and a sudden jolt followed. For a moment, we thought it was the end. We could not see a thing in the cellar, which was full of smoke or dust. Plaster fell on our heads. Someone called to God for help.

After a few seconds, I began to find my bearings. The cellar was not destroyed or buried, so for now we were safe. We remained there; we had nowhere to hide. Our courtyard was covered with beams and other debris from the partly ruined house and did not offer any refuge. Several people chose to run over to other houses. Again, we heard the humming of a plane engine and another whistle. A large bomb exploded on our street, shattering a tall house to its very foundations. Someone said that a couple more jolts like that would be enough to destroy our house, and we'd be buried underneath it. We decided to leave as soon as the raid was over. We considered the things left in the apartment to be as good as lost; having survived such great danger, we did not worry about them.

When at last the bombing stopped, we could see the extent of the destruction: the upper part of the house had been cut off by a bomb falling at an angle. Needless to say, a minute correction in the aiming device of the plane would have meant the complete destruction of the house. This was the silver lining to the cloud, as it were. Mother did not want me to go upstairs to see what state our things were in, but I began to climb up without her permission. I felt a bit like a rat on a sinking ship, since the house could collapse any minute, but motivated by bravery as much as by curiosity, I did not give up. To my surprise, the things were unharmed, if one didn't count a layer of dust. The apartment, however, was seriously damaged: doors and windows were torn out of the embrasures, the wardrobes had toppled, and so forth. I took some of our things, and we made our new abode in a shelter dug in a nearby garden. I was so terrified by the bombings that, once in the shelter, I did not want to leave it.

Everything was quiet. The raids had stopped, and even the street traffic was minimal. A couple of trucks loaded with machines stopped near the garden. They seemed to be evacuating a factory—on the first day of the war? That was what it was: the Germans were approaching in seven-league boots. It was about noon when Mietek came with the news that Germans had taken Kowno. "They can be in Wilno any time now," he said. "We can't stay in the garden, after all!" He was right. We decided to move with all our things to Weglowa 17. With a primus stove in one hand and a bucket filled with our stuff in another, I looked like a real castaway. From the looks people were giving me, I surmised that that was precisely how they saw me. Suddenly, a large German plane appeared just over our street. It flew by without doing any harm. At night we could hear dense machine gun fire.

I finished writing the above memoirs on April 10, 1947.

CHAPTER THREE

THE FIRST GERMANS I saw were on motorcycles. They were carrying bouquets of flowers from the Lithuanians who had come out into the streets en masse to greet them. The Lithuanian women were dressed in national costumes, and Lithuanian flags were flying from many buildings. Lithuanian soldiers were ruthlessly murdering the Soviets who had not managed to leave with the retreating army. Eyewitnesses told us later that Lithuanian infantrymen in Wilno pierced Russian children with bayonets. The Germans considered all the workers who had been sent from Russia for forced ("prinudzilowscy") or ordinary labor to be war prisoners. They marched those "prisoners of war" under armed escort through the streets of the city. This was done with much loud shouting and laughter. Those who tried to pass something to the Russians were also pushed in among their ranks and most probably shared their fate: starvation or execution by a firing squad.

The streets were filled with drunken German soldiers. With their German marks, they went about buying up the entire contents of grocery stores, pastry shops, and, most of all, liquor. In Wilenska Street, I saw a Kraut (German soldier) filling up his motorcycle sidecar with one-liter bottles of vodka and pure spirits. Now and then, Russian bombers arrived, but the anti-air defense was very efficient, and the planes went up in flames like candles. I was furious when I saw a German fighter plane taking on three Soviet bombers, and, after three German machine gun series, all three planes fell, in flames. "Flying coffins" was what people dubbed those unfortunate bombers. This is true heroism, people were saying, to fly a plane that was destined to be shot down. Several times a day, the Soviet planes arrived—and were destroyed. "When will they get bored?" people wondered. One bomber luckily "lost" a couple of bombs before being shot down by the Germans. Big bombs. A moment later, tall columns of smoke rose over Wilno: the leather factories on the Wilja were burning. "At last they have succeeded; they know what the Germans need most," commented the optimists.

So far, there was enough food, but long lines were already forming in front of the stores. Pork fat, for instance, was limited to four hundred grams per person. This, in brief, was what the first two days of the German occupation looked like.

We moved back to our ruined apartment on Zawalna Street and passed two calm nights there, sleeping soundly, like in the good old times. Then the first notes appeared on the stores: Entry Forbidden to Jews. Then came the first roundups and deportations for forced labor, the first arrests for no reason.

One day after the arrival of our "liberators," an announcement was posted all over town: Jews are not to walk on sidewalks. I did not follow any of these new anti-Jewish regulations; I walked when and where I pleased, helped, of course, by my looks. Mother, however, abided by the rules, as did most Jews. One person was already missing in the family of our landlord. Germans came to take his son-in-law; they told him to pack a towel and soap. Several hours later, the unfortunate man was no more.

Another day saw the introduction of special signs meant to distinguish Jews from non-Jews: a yellow circle on white background with the letter J in the middle. Not wanting to wear this "badge," I preferred to stay at home. Some of our friends wore the badge, but they covered it with a scarf, as if by accident, or they placed it on the front of a blazer, under the lapel. They covered the sign because they were embarrassed to wear it, but they had it on because they wanted to be officially correct.

One day, early in the morning, when I was still in bed, a Lithuanian policeman came to our apartment and told me and Mietek to go downstairs, supposedly to go to work. Mietek put on the two "patches," one for the front and one for the back and was ready, while I put on only the one in front and absolutely refused to wear the other one, even though Mother begged me to do it for fear of the consequences. I was eager to go without any apprehension. On the contrary, I was motivated by a stupid curiosity: where will they take us to work?

Just then, the concierge walked up to the policeman, whom she knew well, and asked him not to take me away because I was sick. Her "intervention" helped, and I stayed home. The concierge was positively disposed toward our family. Already in the Soviet times, she had warned Father that his illegal trade was being watched and that he ought to be careful. She was on good terms with a couple of Lithuanian policemen, and after several conversations with them, she told us that we should move to the countryside. "The creation of the ghetto is a matter of days," she told us, "and life there will be a nightmare. Jews will be bereft of everything, and they will have to work hard for a piece of dry bread." Of course, none of us believed her. Mietek came back from work only a little tired. They had taken them to the barracks and had given an order to clean. He washed windows and returned home rather pleased because he had expected something worse.

I was horrified by a march I saw through the window. Two hundred elders with long patriarchal beards were walking, surrounded by plainclothes policemen with revolvers in their hands. We did not realize then that these people were being led to their deaths, but the sight, nonetheless, made a terrible impression on me. It was simply sickening: old men incapable of escaping, with revolvers pointed at their heads. Such marches took place more and more often, but instead of old men, there were now younger men, and the plainclothes policemen were replaced by regular police, wearing their green Lithuanian uniforms and with guns ready to shoot. For the time being, the Germans took little part in the persecution of the Jews. They were the legislators, not the executors. The Lithuanians, on the other hand, turned out to be more than zealous in the execution of their masters' orders. Thousands of Lithuanians joined the Gestapo, most of them former Komsomol members, in order to rehabilitate themselves in the eyes of the Germans. But, in fact, the Germans did not persecute those who had collaborated with the Soviet authorities. On the contrary, those people all retained their posts. I could not believe the speed with which the Lithuanians were changing colors, and now, instead of the Soviet five-armed star, they wore small swastikas on their lapels.

The rumors about the creation of the ghetto were more and more frequent. There were even noises about its eventual site. But what we were hearing varied. "We should have stayed on Weglowa Street; that's where the ghetto will be. You will see. Those people will be lucky. They'll get to stay in their own houses and won't have to schlep their stuff around," Mietek would say. I thought that he was not to be trusted and suspected him then and earlier as well. Sometimes Mother and I wondered whether he wasn't Mrs. Paprocka's accomplice in Father's arrest and its consequences. In the meantime, Mietek was already planning his life in the ghetto: "I will sign up to be in the police to make a living. I'll manage somehow."

As for me, I could not understand at all *why they were telling me to go to some ghetto.* I tried to push this thought as far away as possible, but it returned of its own accord, along with the nearing date of the forcible removal to the ghetto. Posters on city walls announced the new order.

"That's all very well, but how will they fit so many people in such a small area?" people asked; the area designated for the ghetto was the old Jewish neighborhood, which been built for very few inhabitants. The Germans and the Lithuanians managed to do the impossible: in that tiny area they settled not only all the Jews from Wilno but also from the region—two hundred thousand people in all. These butchers had "great" methods, to which I'll return later. Thus the ghetto began to take on a real shape, and several days later, we were supposed to be behind its walls. Some people speculated that, with the creation of the ghetto, there would be no more deportations, arrests, forced labor, etc., or that we would have our own self-government. They believed that the Germans would have to treat us differently. People also said that there would be food shortages, so it was imperative to take as much food as possible, especially fat, with us.

The tailor who was making me a suit said, "Just as I sew here, I shall sew in the ghetto." He represented the view of the majority of the people. Our innate Jewish optimism pushed away any thought of danger that loomed there. This was beneficial because we had no other option anyhow. The ghetto awaited us ...

Jan and Halina Plater-Zyberk arrived unexpectedly. Even before they told us why they had come, we began to feel hopeful. "Your husband promised to take care of my family if something happened to me, and I promised him the same," Jan said with a kind smile. "During the deportations, we were hiding on a farm near Wilno, and we're still there. I believe that you, too, would feel well there, and there is no reason to stay here any longer. The farmer is a clever and brave man; he knows the village administrator and can influence him. I have spoken to him, and he is willing to take you in."

We couldn't find words to thank him. Only now, in light of this new hope, did we realize what a nightmare the ghetto would be. *No! We shall not go to the ghetto! We will live carefree in the countryside.* I was already imagining a vacation in a beautiful garden with kind hosts who would hide us till the end of the war. The farmer was supposed to come the following day to tell us how and when he would move us and our possessions.

The next day was spent waiting. When the farmer didn't show up by noon, we were convinced we were lost. "He won't come. He's afraid because it's too late. If this were at least one day earlier, he'd come, but this is the deadline for going into the ghetto, so he's given up. He's afraid to fall in the hands of the Germans by helping us at a time when the area will be full of Germans sniffing around," we thought.

Having lost hope, we began to see our situation in dark colors.

"They will torture and kill us there. Why did the Platers bother coming at all? There is no other way for us, and now we have to suffer even more!"

The following day, the awaited farmer came at last. He turned out to be also the owner of furniture moving vans. After a few words of introduction, he said simply and to the point, "For twenty thousand rubles, I'll keep you through the war." That was a huge sum of money at the time, but according to Mietek's calculations, the price of a one-carat diamond used to be fifteen hundred rubles, which now must be fifteen hundred marks, that is, fifteen thousand rubles. Hence he did not think this was too much. "One carat and a couple of thousands," he thought. Thus the "price" was agreed upon, and the next day, the farmer was supposed to come to get us and our belongings. These were truly the last moments of surviving outside of the ghetto.

The farmer arrived in the morning with a large wagon. Our things had been packed and ready for a long time. We had a lot of them: the entire wagon was filled with suitcases and sacks. My little sister, who had come back from Olkienniki, and I sat on the heap of our luggage, and soon we were on our way out of the courtyard and into the street. My heart felt light, as if I were coming out of prison. Subconsciously I felt calm; I believed that we would make it safely to our destination. Mother was walking on the sidewalk beside the wagon, naturally without any "patches." Mietek walked way ahead of us. He was elegantly dressed and also without any "signs," as there was a general conviction that Germans looked more favorably upon people who were well-dressed.

After we crossed practically the whole city and were nearing its edge, we saw that Mietek was greeting someone. As it turned out later, this was someone who had once worked with Mietek. He told Mietek that the toll-gates were guarded by Germans who were checking documents. In the same breath, he offered to show us a way around the toll-gates. My sister and I got off the wagon, which continued on a different road. Once we reached the highway, we were supposed to meet up with it. In the meantime, the four of us took a path next to the radio station, shown to us by Mietek's acquaintance. After a quarter of an hour, without any difficulty, we reached the main highway, which we were now supposed to follow for another nine kilometers to Bukiszki, our refuge.

The farmer, who rode with our things and without whose help we could not find the farm, did not appear for a long time. We were very anxious that he might have been stopped with our belongings. Whenever we heard an approaching car, Mietek would hide, so as not to attract attention with his Semitic looks and thereby betray himself and us. At last, the wagon with our stuff appeared, and we felt much relieved.

Soon we turned onto a country road. We were passing wealthy farms, so-called "colonies." Krupowicz was now bringing us to his wooden house, which stood far away to the side. The Platers came out to greet us. On the side of the house, there was a vegetable garden; farther on, one could see fields of grain. Near the barn, there was a young grove, while in the distance we saw the forest. The air was like a balm: clean and fragrant. Empty milk cans were drying upside-down on the fence, and a young heifer strolled calmly through the yard. All this seemed like paradise in comparison with Wilno and what had awaited us there. The farmer's wife served us some cold milk, which tasted like ambrosia, since we had not drunk milk in weeks. I spent the first night in the barn. It was very cold there, and neither Mietek nor I could fall asleep. Mother and my little sister had a bed made in the room. Mother told me later that she hadn't slept that well in a long time. We felt very upbeat. It seemed to us that war did not affect us any longer, that we were beyond its reach. Danger receded into infinity.

One room was placed at our disposal. We put all of our things there and settled in. Soon our hosts told us that we should buy vegetables elsewhere because they didn't have enough for sale. Other products, such as eggs, milk, and potatoes, they could offer us in exchange for things. That same day, Mr. Krupowicz demanded that we pay for our stay. Since we did not have cash, we gave him two diamonds (whose price was not exactly what Mietek had estimated) totaling three carats and a heavy gold cigarette case. Krupowicz, however, did not think that was sufficient and asked that we add the rug. As this was above and beyond what he had agreed upon earlier, we were outraged. Mother told him that she didn't know with what she was going to buy bread, so she couldn't give away all of her valuables. We turned to Jan Plater to be the arbiter in this case, but he refused. In the end, Krupowicz got the rug. When I thought about this haggling later, I could not help but laugh at our inflexible position in regard to the silly rug. Later, I understood that material goods were completely worthless and sometimes constituted an obstacle. It was precisely material goods that led to the downfall of the people who did not have enough fortitude to part with them. After some time, Jan explained to us that he did not want to become involved in the matter out of fear that, without obtaining what he wanted, Krupowicz might take us back to Wilno, where we would perish.

News from Wilno was grim. Mass arrests; people disappearing into another world. Entire families were taken to Lukiszki (the central Wilno prison) and from there to Ponary, a wooded suburb, where deep pits were dug to accommodate the bodies of the executed unfortunates. Children were thrown in alive and covered with dirt; they didn't want to waste bullets on children. All this information came from people who had miraculously escaped from the site of the executions. Every day, we would hear about thousands of people shot to death. For some time seven thousand people a day were taken to Ponary. On a single day, an entire neighborhood of the old town was "liquidated" in the area where the ghetto was to be. Only then did it become clear exactly how the Germans were planning to deal with the huge numbers of people in the ghetto. The place of the former inhabitants was taken by the newly transplanted Jews from Wilno and its surroundings. There was always too little space in the ghetto, so the executions of the former inhabitants continued. Then things calmed down a bit. At that point, our host, Krupowicz, said, "The Germans killed all the poor people because they were afraid of diseases, and they couldn't profit from them in any way. They won't do any harm to rich people because they'll be able to get money from them." Listening to these remarks, we were happy that we had made it to Bukiszki.

The news from the front was that the Germans were unable to continue toward Smolensk and even that they were retreating. Waves of German bombers passed over our heads on their way to the front. Every time I heard the buzz of an airplane engine, I would run outside, wanting to believe that perhaps this one was Soviet. There had been one Soviet air raid on Wilno, and everyone was expecting a bigger one. All this caused us to live in a state of pleasant anticipation. In our imagination, we were already picturing the Soviet army liberating us. *Oh, why didn't they deport us! we thought to ourselves,* and we envied all those who had been deported to the Soviet Union. I would have given anything to be with my family somewhere in deep Russia. We were beginning to understand why my grandmother wrote from Warsaw that she envied our relatives who were in exile near Archangielsk. Earlier, we had laughed at her. We had fantasized then that the "tovarishche" ("comrades"—soldiers of the Soviet Army) were on their way to free us. But Jan said that their return would not be good for Poland, and Halina seconded him. The Krupowicz family was of the same opinion, while we, of course, dreamed of the return of the Soviets.

We obtained food through barter. Most of the time, however, it was hard to get, and I walked around hungry, as even a piece of bread was difficult to find. A pair of pants, for instance, could be exchanged against two kilograms of fat. For a tablecloth, Mother obtained half a pood of bread, that is, about eight kilograms. We bought vegetables at the neighboring state farm where there was an agricultural school. We would go there every couple of days to buy fresh carrots, parsley, celery, and leeks, as well as rhubarb and raspberries, which we had to pick ourselves.

The Krupowiczes had three daughters: Marysia, Zuzia, and Jagoda. The latter was still an adolescent, while the two former were young women and not at all unattractive. They both were partial to the manager and the secretary of the state farm. These men were young Lithuanians, former Komsomol activists, who now, like most of their compatriots, became rabid Nazis. One day, I noticed a swastika painted in the Lithuanian colors on the secretary's notebook. This "color change" was typical of the Lithuanians.

Mother went shopping to the state farm as well, while Mietek sat at home like a mouse and read books. Every day, we would help the farmer's wife cut chaff and in other farm chores. At that time, the Platers left for an estate they owned in Belarus, where they had lived before the war. After their departure, the Krupowiczes' attitude toward us changed for the worse. They demanded horrendously high prices for food, and, now and then, arguments erupted over nothing.

Mother and I began to go frequently to a little village called Jerozolimka. We had friends there—the Dynenson family and the Wajdenfelds, parents of my schoolmate Tadek Wajdenfeld. The Dynensons did not hide their Jewish identity. They believed that by living in such a small village, they would be spared the ghetto. Their hostess, the owner of the villa where they were living, had them pay her in gold rubles, and every month the price of the "rent" increased.

The Wajdenfelds, on the other hand, had changed their last name to Mankowski and were very optimistic, despite their Semitic features. Mr. Wajdenfeld had managed to obtain false papers for his family. As far as I remember, those were Karaim papers, and with them he walked around Wilno without any "patches." He was a very clever and courageous man. Eager to find out what the conditions were really like in the ghetto, he went there himself. What he saw there was horrifying: people were crowded in the streets because there was no room for them anywhere else. Now and then, the Lithuanians caught these unfortunates and delivered them to Ponary.

Sharing the Dynensons' apartment was their brother-in-law, who also wanted to get Karaim papers, and the "bald captain," which was what I called the little retired captain with no hair. This bald captain, a Pole, helped the Dynensons and their brother-in-law in everything. He did this without any ulterior motives. The Karaim papers that the captain was supposed to arrange were all the better because the Karaim, a Jewish religious minority, had Semitic features, but were not persecuted in this area by the Germans. Nonetheless, it was almost impossible to obtain these Karaim documents. We knew that for Mietek, those would have been the best.

Three weeks had passed since we had arrived in Bukiszki. Now and then, I would go to the forest to fetch wood with Krupowicz. I also went mushroom picking with his daughters; we would leave the house with empty baskets and return with splendid boletus mushrooms. Despite that, we could sense that our hosts' attitude toward us was deteriorating. We felt that they did not want us to remain there any longer, but we tried not to think about this because we had nowhere to go. One day, the two elder daughters came home from their daily dalliance with the Lithuanians on the state farm, and they spoke to their parents. Soon thereafter, Mrs. Krupowicz told us that they could not keep us there any longer because the two Lithuanians next door already knew that there was a Jewish family in hiding here.

Without any other possible refuge, the ghetto was the only place to go. It was supposed to close soon, and then this last "shelter" too would be beyond reach. Mother was ready to go to this place of martyrdom. On her knees she would cry and say, "We must carry this cross, this hump. We will follow the path of all other Jews; after all there are thousands of them already there." And Mietek would add, "They won't kill everybody, just the poor; we'll manage somehow," and he, too, was ready to go to the ghetto under the condition that Krupowicz would take our things back to the city and smuggle them into the ghetto. Mrs. Krupowicz added as a consolation that she would throw us some bread across the gate from time to time.

Just listening to this made me sick to my stomach. I realized what going to the ghetto meant: it meant *the end*, and there was no other solution. Wishing to be alone, I went to a secluded spot in the young woods. Next to it, there was a narrow strip of a field and more woods. The wind was quite strong; it tousled my hair. I felt a need to pray. I prayed and, in my prayer, expressed a terrible will to live; I begged for life. *Why am I so miserable and so humiliated? Why do they want to destroy me, to torture me, why?* I closed my eyes and imagined that all this was just a dream, that times were normal again, and all this horror was only a dream. I made an effort to wake up from the dream. I thrashed about; I even pinched my cheek. I opened my eyes and thought that I had woken up from the horrible dream. I looked at the sky; I looked at the harvested grain; and I thought that all this was identical to the reality of my dream. That lasted for a few sweet moments, and then, again, all I could see was the abyss. I knew that ordinary strength would not help here. Here only a higher power could help: *God*. And I had to offer God something in return. My lips said it before I could think, "I will be chaste," and immediately afterward, "Never in my life will I have a woman other than my wife." Such was my first prayer, full of strength and faith. I felt strengthened by it and made up my mind not to go to the ghetto.

Our visits to Jerozolimka brought us false birth certificates and a change of my last name in the school ID. In place of the letter *Y*, a chemist friend of Mr. Wajdenfeld inserted a *U*. From then on we were called the *Dunin* family instead of the *Dynin* family. The false birth certificates for my mother and my little sister were also under that name. We paid for those documents with two gold chains. These papers were not sufficient to have us registered as Poles, but "Half a loaf is better than no bread."

Mother cried very often and kept asking me to agree to go to the ghetto with her; she would kiss me and say, "Jurinku, we are drowning; we are going under; we will perish! I want to follow the official way, otherwise, I'm afraid."

"I won't go to any ghetto," I would answer. "Go without me." I said that, knowing well that she would never leave me. When I thought about it, sometimes I, too, wondered whether it might not be a bad idea to go to the ghetto after all, since here we were sure to die, while there seemed to be a chance there (but a chance of what?). These were the moments in which my reason deceived me and whispered: *Go, go. You will manage somehow … somehow …* Those were the fatal promptings of the perennial Jewish optimism: No, they won't kill us. They've killed others, and now they won't kill any more. Then there was a different commandant; then the Lithuanians had more autonomy … That was our war-enemy number two: the optimism, our curse that destroyed thousands.

In the end, I forgot about my pious decisions, and under the barrage of Mother's and Mietek's insistence, the perennial "somehow we will manage" won me over. In my mind, I was already at peace with the thought of going to the ghetto. I followed the path of least resistance and said to myself, "Whatever will be, will be." We had very little money, and what we had spent on the birth certificates would have been very useful now.

Even though it was already late, I decided to walk to Jerozolimka, a distance of five kilometers, to try to sell back our birth certificates. We wanted to get back at least some money. The road to Jerozolimka was very beautiful. I thought that I would have appreciated this beauty with greater peace of mind if, for instance, I were not Jewish. As it was, it seemed indifferent to me. I crossed through woods and climbed hills, thinking all the time: *Why is this beautiful world created for others and not for me?* If a lovely view was to be seen from one spot, I purposefully avoided it; that's not for me, I thought; that doesn't exist. For me, ahead of me is some void, toward which I was walking in terror and which would swallow me. But other thoughts running through my head were that, somehow, we would manage.

I closed my eyes and thought, once again, that this was all a dream. Reality was so terrifying that it could not be real: I was going to sell the birth certificates in order to go to the ghetto—it had to be a dream! After all, these two could not coexist: my road to annihilation and the beauty of nature. I could not comprehend it. *Why? What had I done? Was this right?* My head was splitting with all these thoughts.

Each minute on the road added new contrasting thoughts and fantasies. I was almost in Jerozolimka. Mr. Wajdenfeld was not in, but I found his son Tadek and his wife at home. I explained to them our situation and the fact that we had no choice but to go to the ghetto. They were absolutely against it. "Chigryn, with his Semitic features, has no other option, but you, your mother, and your sister should take advantage of the value of your looks," they said. This injection of healthy realism encouraged me and made me renew my erstwhile vows. I went back on the "road of the cross" (that was how Mother referred to the road to Jerozolimka later, because of the suffering that made us take it), and I arrived safely in Bukiszki. I recounted my visit to Jerozolimka and again objected to going to the ghetto. While I had gone there and back, Mother had packed all the things she intended to take with us to the ghetto. She had made up her mind that we were going and did not want to hear anything else.

I felt drawn to Jerozolimka again. I felt that I had to return there that very day. I was tired and hungry, but not hearing an inner voice that would tell me, *Go tomorrow. Sleep now. Things will arrange themselves somehow,* I set out on my way. The road was reasonably well-lit, the starry sky and the moon illuminated the countryside. In the distance, there were heavy clouds bringing a downpour. I knew the road by heart—"the road of the cross." But hope that this time I would get help in Jerozolimka pushed me on. I walked as fast as I could; I ran down hills, and soon I was in Mr. Wajdenfeld's apartment. He had come back in the meantime and told me at once that the Dynensons *were no more.* "They were taken from here to Ponary." All the Jews from Jerozolimka had met the same fate. When the Dynensons learned of the planned "action," they hid in the nearby woods, but, unfortunately, the Lithuanians managed to catch them there. That was so strange— they had been free until recently, and now they had been tortured and led to their death. For what? Of course, just as I had suspected, Mr. Wajdenfeld was of the opinion that we must not go to the ghetto under any circumstances. I didn't even mention the idea of selling our birth certificates. I had made up my mind to fight and not, as others did, go to the slaughter like so many sheep.

When I walked back, the sky was covered with clouds. It was completely dark. I walked as if blindfolded. Halfway, I ran into a Lithuanian patrol. I recognized them by their jockey caps. It was truly strange that they did not stop me. I was lucky. At last, I made it to the courtyard of Krupowicz's farm.

First, I recounted the tragedy that had befallen the Dynensons. In reply, I was told that they were taken to Lukiszki, a well-known prison and the first stop on the way to Ponary, because they had been caught in the woods; if they had come of their own accord, they would have been taken to the ghetto, not to prison.

I knew well that that made no sense, because people sent to Lukiszki and from there to Ponary were not guilty of anything. Their only fault was that they were Jewish. I was irritated by the perpetual self-deception practiced by my family and told them in no uncertain terms that we would never go to the ghetto. I felt a power within me, and I influenced my family with its help. It was as if I had become the head of the family, and Mother relied on me for leadership.

The following morning the Krupowicz family expected a visit from the soltys (the head of the village) and the manager of the state farm. Early in the morning, Mother and I went to the forest for the entire day so as not to be seen by them. Mietek hid in the barn, and my little sister stayed at home. Mother and I sat down on tree trunks in a coniferous forest. We had brought some food with us. I felt very safe there, but the idea of returning to the farm filled me with anxiety. Krupowicz had promised us that he would signal the departure of the officials by appearing in the doorway facing the forest. So we sat in the forest thinking about our situation. We realized that our stay with the Krupowicz family was as good as finished and that we had to find another refuge. On the way back, we passed by peasant huts standing in gardens: they looked positively bucolic.

"Why can't we rent such a hut under the name Dunin?" I asked Mother. But I agreed with her that that would have been too close to the Krupowiczes, who would then know our whereabouts and whom we no longer trusted. When we approached the farm, I was able to tell with my sharp eyes that no one was standing in the doorway, so the "guests" must have been still inside. We entered a small grove by the road and awaited the chance of returning to the house. The day was almost over, and we were getting impatient. It was impossible that they would be there so long. "I'll go by myself to check the situation," I said. And that was what I did. When I was closer to the house, I heard

Mietek's voice—proof that the way was clear. I called Mother, and we went into the house.

The following day brought us to a decision. In Jerozolimka we ran into Andrzej Plater, Jan's brother. Anio, as he was called, advised us to go to Belarus in the footsteps of his older brother. The address he gave us was "Sworotwa near Nowogrodek." We held on tight to this idea, and from then on, all our efforts were directed toward Sworotwa. We had to get there.

When the Krupowiczes asked us where we intended to go, we answered that we were going to the Platers'. They received the news with indifference. Only the three of us—Mother, my little sister, and I—could go to the Platers'. Mietek, with his looks, could not undertake such an escapade. The Krupowiczes agreed to keep Mietek with them. Mrs. Krupowicz gave him a medallion with the Madonna, which Mietek kissed fervently and put on his neck. Thus our separation from Chigryn was decided.

We took with us the things that had been readied earlier, for going to the ghetto. Mother left Mietek a diamond. All we had left was one diamond, the last remaining jewel, the only thing we could sell. The rest of the jewelry, hidden in the mirror and in the bootjack, could not be liquidated. An attempt to sell any of those pieces could raise suspicions, since those objects were very valuable. Mietek claimed that he did not have anything of value, and to leave him like that would have been inhuman, we reasoned. In any case, we did not need anything; after all, we were going to an estate where we would have everything for free. We might just need a little money for the road, and that we could get by selling our last diamond. We were thinking of how to escape from the Wilno area. We were convinced that horrible things were happening only in Wilno, where the Lithuanians were ruling. Naturally, we intended to change places, but remain under the name Dunin, that is, as Poles. The things that we were going to take with us to the Platers' Krupowicz took to his Wilno apartment and from there moved them to an apartment belonging to the Platers' friends, the Milejkos. We made our final good-byes with Bukiszki, and we went to Jerozolimka, the first stop on our journey. Mother and my little sister left first, and I followed about an hour later, in order not to attract anyone's attention. We imagined that three people walking might arouse suspicions. In Jerozolimka, we met up with Anio again, and he introduced us to the Milejkos. We sent my little sister, Dzidzia, at once to their Wilno apartment.

We had to spend one night in Jerozolimka. We went to a villa with Miss Milejko, who introduced us, of course, as the Dunins to the owner. Worried that it might seem suspicious if we stayed for one night only, we claimed that we were interested in renting a room for the entire winter. We gave the woman a small down payment, I asked a few questions about firewood, and we began our "wintering" there. The following morning, we left. Mother forgot some of her clothes there and, of course, we did not go back to get them. Our hosts must have thought us strange to have paid a down payment, left a part of our wardrobe there, and never returned. Our planned route to the Platers' continued through Wilno.

Before nightfall, I boarded a ship on the Wilja going to Wilno. Naturally, there was a sign on board: No Entry for Jews. They checked documents selectively to make sure there were no Jews. No one asked to see my papers, which meant that I had "good" looks. On board, I noticed two Polish high school friends of mine. I did not want them to see me, so I went to the lower deck. Upon arrival, I also waited until they got off and were some distance away before I left the ship. From there, I went to the apartment of the Zachorski family, with whom Anio was living. Both the Zachorskis and the Milejkos knew exactly who we were. By taking us in, they were exposing themselves to great danger. Mother arrived in Wilno the following day. Our next task was to figure out how to leave Wilno. We found out that, every morning, a car left for the Pienocentras dairy cooperative. The car went by the Wielkie Soleczniki estate. That was on the road from Lidy to Nowogrodek, so in the direction that suited us. There was no other transportation at the time. We decided to leave the following day.

We ate dinner in a restaurant in the city. There were several

German soldiers there as well. One of them was playing jazzy pieces on the piano. This would have been quite pleasant if not for the fact that we were convinced people were observing us. Unwittingly, I was acting strangely in order to replicate the manners of a pure Pole. Mother, feeling the same way, was also acting unnaturally. It was with relief that we left the place. Mother went to see how Dzidzia was doing, and I went back to the Zachorskis' apartment. On my way, I ran into Dmowski—the man who had not returned several precious objects after Father's arrest. He walked up to me, started kissing me, and told me that he was delighted to see me alive. Was I not afraid to walk in the streets like that? After all, I could run into a Pole who knew me and could denounce me.

I told him that I had no need to fear my friends. "Watch out, watch out!" he bade me good-bye. I didn't even mention his debt. A friend from school, one with whom I had shared a desk, passed me by and didn't even look at me, as if I had the plague. The night passed by in peace.

Mother and I stayed in the large room of the Zachorskis' apartment. I could not sleep after all. I was thinking anxiously of the day to come. In addition, the busy traffic in the street didn't let me close my eyes. The following morning at dawn, we said good-bye to the Zachorskis. We went to the place where the Pienocentras cars left from. We made arrangements with the driver that, on the way, he would stop to pick up Dzidzia and the luggage. The driver agreed to this very unwillingly, and to make matters worse, Mother missed the house where Dzidzia was staying, and we had to drive back a good bit. The driver said he would wait only a few minutes.

When I went upstairs to get my little sister, she was not dressed yet. She got dressed very quickly, and I began to take the luggage down. I carried two suitcases to start. I asked the Milejkos for help because the driver was getting impatient and was honking in the street. They refused. I had to kick my backpack down the stairs because my hands were full of other things. A great thermos pot containing honey bought in Bukiszki for barter stayed upstairs. The servant, whom I also asked for help in taking it down, didn't answer at all and stood like a mummy, glad that at least this little "souvenir" would be left behind "after the Jews." When at last we were in the car with our things, a load was lifted off my chest. I felt carefree and safe, without any fears. We passed the city, past Zawalna Street and past the gates of the ghetto. The Lithuanian police stood by the entrance and the exit from the ghetto.

When we left the ghetto behind, my mood improved even more. We were finally going to leave this cursed city! We were again free, and, once we had crossed the Lithuanian border, we would be completely free—that is what we were thinking. I analyzed the last scenes I had witnessed in the streets of Wilno. There were the "Chosen People," going to the ghetto. A half-dead horse was pulling a cart filled with bundles and things; the road headed uphill, and the horse stopped every few steps. It had to pull things and people who were so feeble that they were holding on to the cart in order to get a bit of a lift on the way up. In this group, I saw a young, good-looking, blond man, carrying a backpack. He did not look at all like a Jew. He could hide instead of marching with others like sheep for slaughter, I thought. Another image: a Gestapo officer in uniform, escorting a poor Jewish family into the ghetto. The real criminal was walking on the sidewalk, while the ostensible "criminals" were walking in the street, poorly dressed and with few packages. They looked completely resigned, indifferent. Some Germans standing nearby burst into laughter. The Gestapo officer also laughed and said something to his "brothers." A young man whom I recognized as a graduate of the Epsztajn Middle School was taking Germans around from one liquor store to another. (He's made "friends.") All this made a dreadful impression on me, even though this was before we had a chance to get to know the Germans fully.

A man in his thirties had come to see us a few days after the German entry into town. His name was Narwoja—a Lithuanian. He told us that he was taken away on the same train as my father and that he knew where Father was. He also promised to bring us some food. We gave him money; he returned with food. The second time we gave him more money for food, he did not come back. He reappeared after a while to tell us that he would go to look for my father, but he needed money. Of course, this time we gave him none. I ran into a high-school friend who was working, paving the street. During the Soviet rule, he was a member of the Komsomol. He asked me bitingly when I would be leaving for Lublin. (Lublin was the place of deportation of many Jews.)

Wilno, the city that cost us so many tears and pain, was behind us. We'll never go back there, we said to ourselves. We were going to a place where we would wait out the war in peace. In the meantime, the car was picking up more and more passengers. Without having been stopped even once, we arrived at Wielkie Soleczniki. The car would not go any farther. Our route was through Lida, so we had to find a means of getting there next. For a piece of leather, a wagon gave us a lift to a village halfway to Lida. Several peasant women walked up to us and asked where we were from. I said that we were from Warsaw, to which they replied, "Surely your father is an officer who is a POW." We confirmed this. "Stay in our village," they said. "We already have one family like this, and we take up collections for them. Everyone gives some staples and some money. Stay with us. There will be enough for you as well." We thanked them warmly for the invitation, but we declined.

For a pair of trousers, we hired a wagon that took us farther. We were going very slowly, and at dusk, we arrived in a little town about four kilometers before Lida. Instead of patches, Jews here wore an armband with two Stars of David. We asked in the street where we might spend the night. They pointed to a Jewish inn. This was the first time we played our comedy in front of Jews. They asked, "What's happening in Wilno?" I recounted the entire horror of the situation in which Jews found themselves there. We concluded together that this was all the fault of the Lithuanians, whom the Germans had given carte blanche. We slept soundly. The innkeepers helped arrange another wagon for us, and, as a result, a very decent peasant drove us farther. He told us how he pitied the Jews and hated the Germans. We crossed through Lida. Jews were taking apart the remnants of the burned town. The entire center had been burned. The peasant told us that the

Germans burned the center on purpose because only Jews lived there and that was where they had all their stores. We left Lida behind us.

Slowly we came to the bridge over the Niemen. It was not easy to find another wagon. No one wanted to leave their fireside. At last, one villager agreed to take us in return for six poods of grain or for its equivalent in cash. We were sure that, since we were going to an estate, nothing would be easier to get than six poods of grain. What is a sack of grain for an estate? We went through an ancient forest. We inhaled the fresh forest air.

We forgot about Wilno entirely—no one bothered us, and there were no Germans to be seen anywhere. The silence, the hum of the wind, and the pleasant coolness of the air made us dream. We heard a few shots in the distance. "This must be our count, hunting," said Mother.

I remember Jan's hunting stories—various tales, some rather fantastic, but to which I always listened with attention as politeness demanded. "Perhaps this is indeed he who was shooting," I said to Mother. "He's probably doing nothing but horse-back riding," I added.

"You'll learn how to ride well," said Mother.

As we were approaching our goal, our thoughts were becoming more and more optimistic. There was still a good bit to go before Molczadz. Our peasant did not know the road very well, and we had to ask for directions very often. Once, I asked a peasant woman if she had heard of the Platers. "They're the ones in Sworotwa," she said.

"That's right," I said.

"Three kilometers from here," she added unexpectedly.

"How can that be? We are only fifteen kilometers from Molczadz, and from there it's still a good bit," I said.

"Near Molczadz is Little Sworotwa, and the one, where the Platers are, is Great Sworotwa" was her answer.

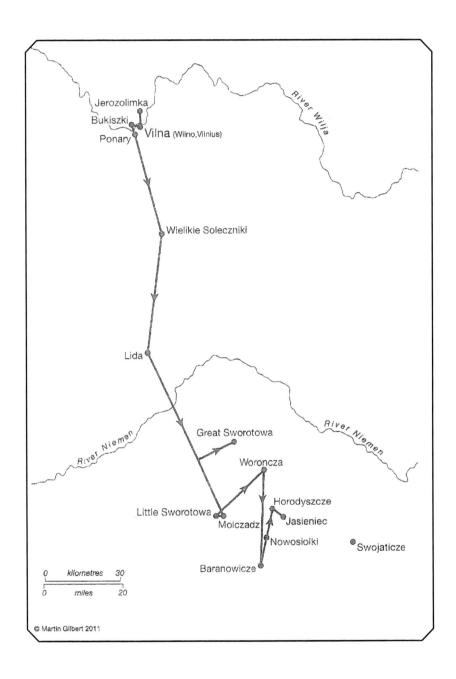

Jerozolimka

Bukiszki

Ponary

Vilna (Wilno, Vilnius)

River Wilia

Wielikie Soleczniki

Lida

River Niemen

River Niemen

Great Sworotowa

Woroncza

Horodyszcze

Little Sworotowa

Jasieniec

Molczadz

Nowosiolki

Swojaticze

Baranowicze

0   kilometres   30

0   miles   20

© Martin Gilbert 2011

CHAPTER FOUR

WE WERE VERY NEAR to the goal of our journey. From afar, we could see a tall tower, which appeared from the distance like a turret of an old castle. At last, we arrived at the gate of the Great Sworotwa estate. The count and the countess received us without much enthusiasm. Halina was filled with consternation at the arrival of such unexpected and, moreover, not "kosher" guests. Her face became pale, and immediately after greeting us, she said, "Unfortunately Janek is not the manager of the estate; we arrived too late and someone else had taken his place. We own a little barter store, and that's how we make a living. We will send you to Wyszek (Jan Plater's brother) in Swojatycze. That is a large estate, of which he's the manager."

We were told all this before we even entered the vestibule of the little white house that used to be occupied by the gardener. That was where the count and the countess lived now. Jan was sitting at the table and working on some accounting. He smiled at us by the way of a greeting, and I could see how he swallowed in terror at such guests. He soon explained to me the nature of his little business. He was bringing paints, shoe wax, and so forth, from Baranowicze, and, in exchange, he took back various produce and food. We were most disappointed with this state of things. Instead of a rich estate, hunting, and horse-back riding, we found a small store with shoe wax. However, we shook our daydreams off quickly and attended to matters at hand, of which the first one was to pay our peasant. Instead of estate grain, he got German marks from our stock. We ate a meal of delicious scrambled eggs, followed by buttermilk, which tasted great. We were too exhausted by the trip to think of what would come next. We were practically falling asleep at the table and couldn't wait for the evening.

At last, the night arrived with the soft light of a kerosene lamp, which flickered all over the little house. We slept in clean sheets and without any fear; our sleep was deep and free from anxiety. We slumbered until late morning hours, delighting in the newly found safety. It was a sunny autumn day. It was moderately warm outside. The count was respected by the local authorities, that is, the *wojt* (the county administrator) and the police, mostly, Belorussians and Poles. Taking advantage of the circumstances, Halina obtained an ID for my mother. We were in seventh heaven. A real document with a photograph issued in the name Franciszka Dunin, of Polish nationality. Now we had proper documents, as the birth certificates made in Jerozolimka were not proper identification, and we were afraid to show them since they had many inaccuracies. We were supposed to rest a bit at the count's and then decide what to do. There was no more talk of leaving for Swojatycze.

I spent most of my time fishing in a small river that traversed the estate; I also took sunbaths and generally had a grand old time. The countess's kitchen consisted of one daily menu, that is, potatoes with a tiny bit of butter and buttermilk for breakfast, and chicken soup and chicken meat for dinner. In exchange for his goods, the count received mostly domestic birds and eggs. There were always several hundred hens and chickens "in stock." Packed tightly into small coops, they were practically suffocating or starving. There was such overcrowding in these coops that chickens walked on chickens. Every day, we would get rid of the ones that had died, and if one showed the least signs of life, it went directly to the countess's kitchen. Soon we got tired of this chicken menu. Supper was the mirror image of breakfast. Bread was sliced very thinly (aristocratically), which meant that all of the bread on the table was actually not enough for a single person. When now I think of what people had to eat in ghettos and in camps, I see that the count's menu was truly aristocratic. But at the time, I had no idea, and I walked around perpetually hungry. I drowned my hunger in buttermilk. In the evenings, I played chess with the count or helped him with his accounts. Alternatively, we went for walks. The count told me stories from his life, and sometimes, when he entered a kind of trance, he spoke very picturesquely and interestingly, imitating the voices of animals while telling hunting tales.

The manager of the estate was a Mr. Kuraszycki, who, in order to gain the Germans' approval, had taken Belorussian citizenship. The countess warned us against him as against a dangerous and unpleasant man whom we were to avoid at all costs. Mr. Kuraszycki's attitude toward us was sympathetic, but possibly false. In any case, Mr. Kuraszycki "smelled" the aristocrats in us. The countess took the opportunity to drop a hint about our being their distant relatives.

In the area, there were rumors of Jews hiding under Polish names who had been found out. At the least suspicion, the victim was asked to recite a prayer. Sometimes a priest was asked to participate in the examination of the suspects. From that time, Halina supplied us with four basic Catholic prayers in Polish, and we had to learn them by heart. We really liked "Our Father, Who Art In Heaven" because its contents could apply to the Christian as well as to the Jewish religion. That was the prayer we learned the fastest. The countess tried to convince us of the superiority of Christianity over Judaism and of the senselessness of suffering as Jews when we could, once and for all, "let go of the cross" and become Christians, especially since we had the right looks. She insisted above all on christening my little sister. We knew that the Christian religion deems it a great merit to convert "infidels" and that, in this way, the countess was trying to secure a better place for herself in the world to come. We did not ponder the essence of this act because, in our opinion, this event made a very faint impression on us at the time and perhaps had a great meaning for the Platers but not for us. Soon my little sister ostensibly changed her religion from Judaism to Catholicism (in the eyes of Halina), very quietly, at the parish of a priest who was an acquaintance of the countess. Despite her young age, she played her role well, and we, too, put holy medals with the Madonna around our necks to make a more convincing impression as Poles.

On the grounds of the estate, there was a small chapel where the ancestors of the Platers were buried. In 1939, after the Soviets entered that area, the local peasants plundered the chapel in search of gold and precious stones on the corpses. Now, Halina decided to put the chapel in order. The human bones that were strewn all over were to be collected and placed in the coffins again. I did not consider this work to be pleasant, but if someone from our family did not participate in this, it would be considered suspect, since this was deemed a very honorable Christian duty, especially since we were related to the Platers. So, in any case, Mother had to go with the countess to put the graves in order.

There were two Jewish families living at the estate. The dairy worker was the head of one of those families, and the former manager of the mill was the father and the husband in the second family. Both families were living in the same little house, and it seemed that they would be spared the cruelty of the bandits. There was a garden surrounding the house, and in it children played or pulled up vegetables. When once the count wanted to give Mr. Srebny (the ex-miller) a piece of beef, he refused to accept it, saying that as long as he could, he would eat kosher meat, and when there wasn't any, he would come to ask the count for help himself. Since all the Jews had to be employed, Mr. Srebny worked at the estate as a farm hand. When I talked to him about the general situation of the Jews and about what I had seen in Wilno, I asked him what he thought of all that and what his hopes were. He answered that God was his hope. I remember he had a seven-year-old daughter.

Every few days, the region's Landwirt, a German officer on off-front duty who was the agricultural administrator, would come to the estate. His translator was a Jew, a very intelligent man from Warsaw. His family lived in Horodyszcze—a town about twenty kilometers from Sworotwa. The Germans set up their local authorities there. All the German offices for the region were concentrated in Horodyszcze, and it was from there that the Germans would leave for inspections of the area. The Kreislandwirt (the district agricultural administrator) led the count to believe that he would appoint him as the main overseer of the estates near Sworotwa. All we could think of was this grand possibility, because then all the estates of the area would be open to us, and in the end we could settle on one of them. Since it was clear that the war would last a long while, we wanted to become independent and find better conditions. We were tired of the Sworotwa diet, and we did not want to be a burden to the count and the countess any longer. In addition, we thought that it was wise to change places; we were afraid that someone might suspect who we really were, even though we had no reason to believe this.

The count and the countess had a daughter who was my little sister's age. Her name was Roza. We became friends at once and played together all the time. I remember that Roza wore braids and was a very good child, obedient to her parents and very clean.

Every day, the count's former gamekeeper came to visit the count. He always brought a gift—a basket of mushrooms, a head of cheese, and so on. He was a tall, strong man. They called him the American because he had spent many years in America, where he had saved up some money with which he bought a piece of land not far from Sworotwa (two kilometers away). He lived in a house that distinguished itself from others by its size and cleanliness. The countess asked him to rent out a room to us, and he agreed. His place was even more out of the way than Sworotwa itself. The road from Sworotwa led near a young birch grove called the "Pantry" and then crossed a bridge over a river. The house was not in the village, but next to it. Peace and quiet permeated the air. The farmers welcomed us very warmly as the relatives of the count. In the evenings, the farmer discussed politics with us: he was an enemy of the Soviets and a rabid anti-Semite. Life went by peacefully and calmly, just like the surroundings. Mother cooked wonderful soups, mostly mushroom soups because mushrooms abounded there.

In the meantime, threshing began at the estate. A large tractor came to power the threshing machine. Several sacks of grain were filled in a matter of minutes. Jan employed me as a granary manager. I weighed and wrote down the weight of sacks filled with rye, working almost without a moment's break. The threshing promised to go on for a while. Each worker received ten rubles a day (which at the time equaled one mark); a pood of rye cost sixty rubles. This was not very high pay, but I had the satisfaction of holding the red paper (the value of ten rubles) in hand—hard-earned money. I ate at the Platers', and in this way was not a burden to my mother. It was late fall when the threshing came to an end.

In the morning, I would walk through frozen puddles that crackled under my feet. Hoarfrost covered the roofs, and even though it was not winter yet, the village of Sworotwa looked as if it were powdered with snow.

At last came the day long awaited by the count and by us. Soon after he was responsible for the threshing at Sworotwa, the count received the plenipotentiary powers over the Podczapowskie area estates. From then on, I was to accompany Jan in his inspections. Every day, we traveled to various farms and stopped to chat with owners and examine the condition of the buildings and of the livestock. Accompanying the count was very pleasant because, in addition to the pleasure of riding in a good wagon pulled by a strong horse, there was also the fact that everywhere we went, we were received in a "lordly" fashion. Whenever we arrived at an estate for inspection, the estate steward would invite us for a little something. To the table were brought pork fat with eggs, roasted filet of beef, and moonshine.

When I had my very first glass of moonshine, I drank it up gingerly because I remembered that, before the war, I had read about all sorts of poisonings with moonshine and of people going blind. The consequences of the drink were not delayed. I could not hear the conversation any longer; all I heard was a hum, or rather, various hums, most likely originating in the voices of several people. My eyesight became dim, and there was no question whatsoever of my getting up from the chair. I was, however, conscious enough to pinch myself in the hand in order to determine whether I could still feel. "So moonshine is indeed a poison," I thought to myself, and I became terrified that my vision would always be so blurred and that I would not hear clearly ever again. Such were the results of my first drink of moonshine.

It is certain that the conversation between the count and the steward lasted a long time. I determined that I was gradually returning to my normal state. When it got dark, the count stood up and took his leave. I did the same, but with much difficulty; through sheer willpower, I seated myself in the wagon. A moment later, we were on the way home, and it was lovely to take a nap while the wagon jostled me lightly. We were greeted with bitter reproach for having come home late.

On another occasion, we visited the estate Burdakowszczyzna. A grand palace, in which only a few rooms were inhabitable, stood facing the road. Its former splendor and luxury were every bit as apparent as the current poverty and shabbiness of the estate.

The manager of the estate was Mr. Holoszczyc, its former steward. We had to pass a long row of doors in a corridor to get to the steward's room. Having knocked gently, the count walked into the room, and I followed. The tiny room was unbearably stuffy. The air was gray with cigarette smoke, mixed with a smell of old clothes, mold, and … horse. This mixture was so deadly that I had to use all of my will power not to back out of the room. On a dirty sheet on a wooden bed in the middle of the room was Mr. Holoszczyc. He was wearing a sheepskin jacket and boots. A large moustache gave him, perhaps, a touch of the nobleman; he also had very thick brows and pointed yellow cheeks. The count questioned him on matters concerning the estate, which was in a pitiful state. There were eight cows, which altogether gave five liters of milk. The boar had barely enough strength to stand up—and that was not because of the weight of his fat. He was a real skeleton, who used his remaining forces to squeal desperately from hunger. The squeal was heard from a distance, even before one arrived at the estate. Upon departure, we took with us the only kilogram of butter, which the count gave to me. I paid for it the official price of twenty-eight rubles and surprised Mother. Soon, I was familiar with the whole area. I met many people and visited a lot of estates and villages. Everyone treated me with respect because of the perceived relationship to the Platers.

One November day, there appeared in Sworotwa an elderly lady who briefly described her mission. She was hoping to place three Polish boys at the estate. This was an illegal action, so-called "social work," which consisted of strengthening the Polish element in the eastern borderlands. "They" appeared soon after her visit. They were in their early twenties, from the families of middle-class intellectuals. They told stories of difficulties on the road, of how badly they had been received by a parish priest, etc. They were full of life, and their words burst with good cheer. They felt at home at once and treated me as one of them. The conditions at the Platers' became tight. I understood that my stay with them was approaching an end.

On the very night after their arrival, I went to sleep at Mother's. It was completely dark when I walked to the village where Mother was living with my little sister. I was passing near a young grove. On the other side, there was an open field. Not a soul in sight. I wasn't afraid of anything, for I knew that here there could only be a robber in wait, but never someone who would want to check my documents. The former fear had abandoned us completely, while the latter tormented us beyond measure.

Jan decided to keep one of the boys, Stefan Slonimski, with him at the estate. He was tall and blond, the son of a doctor from Warsaw. Tadeusz, the second boy, found a place at the Halinowek estate, where he was well-received by the lady owner and her daughters—which was most important to him, as he later told me. The third arrival, a Pieprzyk from Poznan, went to Mala Sworotwa. When Stefan replaced me at the count's side, we began to ask ourselves what to do next. We were subsisting without any economic basis, and this could not go on, especially since the farmer with whom we were staying was beginning to look askance at our long sojourn. At some point, he told us very gently that the count had requested a room for us for a short time.

Our next refuge was Burdakowszczyzna. We packed our modest belongings onto a wagon, and we set out on the road. Our host drove us himself. Overall, we were very grateful to him for his hospitality. The period spent at his house was a time of breathing freely, and Mother repeated more than once that we would recall it with nostalgia. That was when I would say that I was convinced we would be even happier in the future. During our stay in Andrzejowicze, our playing Aryans had gone very well. In the evenings, Mother and my little sister prayed in such a way that the farmer and his wife could hear their whispers across the wall. Moreover, Mother cooked typically Polish dishes and used idiomatic Polish expressions

Our drive seemed endless. We were delighted when the wagon rolled into the courtyard in front of the palace. Next, we found out that, even though Jan had notified them about our arrival, nothing was ready. The room where we were supposed to stay was occupied by "vostochniks," refugees from the areas formerly belonging to the Soviet Union, who would not hear about moving. Temporarily, we installed ourselves in the room of the steward's assistant, a young teacher by the name of Blasinski. He was aware of our high connections and tried to be kind, but his eyes contradicted his actions. For the time being, we put our things in his room, unpacking only the most necessary objects. We dreamed of our own little place, of a small wardrobe and a bed, and this thought helped us live through the first days there. We hoped that the situation would become normal and that we would be able to settle down there.

After twenty-four hours of dry food, such as bread with pork fat, we were hungry for something hot. All our neighbors had already occupied their spots on the stove, so we had to build some fire ourselves. Mr. Blasinski lent me an ax, or, rather, a tool that had a three-centimeter-thick blade. To make matters worse, the handle was very loose, and every couple of minutes, it had to be adjusted so that the blade would not fly off. I was supposed to chop knotty apple wood with this beauty. The chopping did not go well. Only after several hours of work had I chopped enough wood for the fire. I began making a fire in the tall heating stove in our room. I used up a whole bunch of straw, and I blew with all my strength, and at last, I was rewarded with a tiny golden flame. It was very gratifying to see the fire that was kindled by the sweat of my brow, literally. In the meantime, Mother borrowed a "czogun," a round pot that one could use in the stove. It was chipped and dirty, as if with manure. After a thorough scrubbing, we used it for cooking. The first soup that Mother made with produce we had brought from Sworotwa was delicious. Our mood improved as a pleasant sense of warmth spread all over our bodies. I could feel my feet thawing and looked with pleasure as the face of my little sister became rosy. Our room, where the temperature had been barely at a few degrees Celsius, was now almost bearable. We slept on an old mattress full of holes.

The following morning, we were supposed to assume our duties. Mother was to cook for the "administration," that is, for Holoszczyc and Blasinski, and I was going to manage the dairy. My role was to ensure the cleanliness of the cows during milking, to oversee the feedings, and to keep the books. The latter was not too difficult: of the five liters of milk produced daily, two went to the dairy and three to the administration. When I told the milkmaids that they needed to keep everything clean during the milking—thinking all along that I and my family would be drinking the milk ourselves—they replied that I was obviously eager to show off my power over them and that was why I demanded such "extra" work. After finishing my work with the cows, I went to help Mother. I carried water from the well and chopped wood. Most of the time, Mother made potato soup with milk because there was no other fat. There was only one plate at the estate, so Holoszczyc ate first, then Blasinski, and the three of us ate directly from the czogun.

Soon, we were given a large room—a hall with three tall windows. The ancient floor tiles were almost gone, and the floor was very uneven. Not far from the door there was a small stove, the sole pleasure in our life. The heat was concentrated within a radius of only a couple of meters from the stove. That was where we remained as much time as we could during the moments when we were not working. There was a perpetual problem with firewood. It took us several days to convince old Holoszczyc that he should agree to the cutting down of an old birch tree that he wanted to "keep" for the "return" of the former owners of the estate. After that first birch tree, others followed, and obtaining wood was no longer a problem.

We were always hungry. Meat was not to be seen. Now and then, the countess would send us a hen from their store. Even though we knew that the hen most probably had dropped dead, we ate it, nonetheless, because its origin no longer bothered us. Meantime, the cows stopped giving milk almost completely. Thanks to Jan's intervention, we no longer had to send any milk to the dairy. Old Holoszczyc was very upset because of this, and he shouted that he had to show gratitude to the Germans for having "liberated him from the Bolsheviks," and that was why we should send the milk to the Germans and not drink it. Naturally, I stopped sending the milk away, and with the few liters we were getting, Mother was able to make a little butter from time to time. We had plenty of potatoes because I took care of the key to the cellar where the boar's potatoes were stored. Mother's bread would come out of the oven as flat as a pancake because she had very little experience in baking. Preparing any dish was very hard because everything, from the smallest to the largest thing, had to be borrowed. Thanks to Mother, everybody at the estate liked us and was friendly toward us, and lent us things willingly.

I remember one time when the glass lampshade of the kerosene lamp we had borrowed from the neighbors fell and broke to pieces. At the moment, it seemed that it would have been better to lose all our possessions than to break that lampshade, which could not be replaced for any sum of money. Mother was trying to think of what we could possibly give in exchange for the lampshade, and I was in despair as well, since I knew that we couldn't quarrel with anyone, and the simple matter of the broken lampshade could make enemies out of these people. Fortunately, I found that the lampshade from our old lamp fit. A weight was lifted off our shoulders. We felt light and happy, albeit cold, because it was dark and the stove had died out.

Generally, our life there was hard. Old Holoszczyc found fault with everything we did. He wasn't pleased with anything. He muttered under his breath all the time and now and then yelled out, eager to show his gratitude for the "liberation." One never knew when he was ready to eat. Mother usually hovered about with a plate of soup for him while he prayed fanatically, and when his prayers were done, the soup was cold, and the fire had to be rekindled for it to be reheated.

From time to time, the boar gave us an occasion for some merriment. Peasants would bring their pigs to be "covered," trusting that this boar, by virtue of being at the estate, must be a pure breed. But the "pure breed" did not feel like making love, and when they brought him a sow, he paid no attention to her, but continued to emit his hungry squeal. In the meantime, Mr. Holoszczyc impatiently awaited the news in his smoky room. Blasinski ran back and forth to keep the steward abreast of the progress made by the boar. The question "Has she been covered?" made it seem as if the matter were of utmost importance.

Days went by as we worked, waited for good news from the front— news that never arrived—and complained about our difficult situation, laughed at the old steward's ways, and waited for hot food. Nights were spent sleeping very uncomfortably. There was no bed. Instead, we had an old garden bench with a back. We moved our sack filled with clothes to the side, as a kind of barrier. Still it took a lot of skill not to fall off, as the edge of the bench was rounded.

One day, the snow fell. All the mud, puddles, and trash were covered with a white layer. It was beautiful. The orchard and the fields, the garden and the granaries, everything became white and clean. The lake at the estate iced over. Underneath the ice, we could see fish. Children caught the fish in a curious way: They would hit the ice with an ax in the spot where they saw the fish. The stunned fish then appeared in the hole in the ice. This sport brought a lot of profit, and the people at the estate ate fish much of the winter.

At about that time, we received news of a pogrom in Horodyszcze. The word was that over one thousand Jews had been killed there. Up until then, there hadn't been such a mass slaughter in Belarus. We had thought that something like that could only happen in Wilno because we believed that the Lithuanians were the only ones capable of such murder. After some time, the details of the pogrom reached us.

The Germans demanded that the Jewish committee furnish them with some healthy young men for work. Then they drove these men outside of the town and told them to dig pits. The men never came back. Then the Germans came for a new transport of people for slaughter. The inhabitants of the town understood what was happening, but out of great terror became as if paralyzed and did not resist when they were packed onto trucks and taken to the place of their death. The executions were done by the Germans and the Lithuanians, while the Belorussian police helped to "organize the transport." After that mass murder, the only Jews left in Horodyszcze—a little over one hundred of them—became the specialists. The things belonging to the murdered Jews were sorted and put in storage.

Count Jan, who came to see us shortly afterward, told us that the peasants were saying that the Germans had avenged themselves in Horodyszcze for the fact that, the previous winter, the Jews in Horodyszcze had made a snowman that looked like Hitler and then had thrown snowballs and stones at it until it fell apart. We felt very depressed. Naturally, we did not display our feelings and kept an indifferent exterior, never taking part in the discussions of the massacre, even when someone criticized it.

As for me, I understood that the Germans would not stop with the Jews of Horodyszcze. I thought more and more about the essence of this danger. It was best to think when I was alone. I would go through the park to a little wooden bridge. It was a quiet spot, and no one interfered with my considerations. I had considered myself, Mother, and my little sister safe from the Germans. We were under the protection of the Platers, and everyone knew us as the Dunins. We had begun to adjust to the difficult conditions there and to the inadequate food. We would survive somehow. We had even decided that, when we made it alive through the war, we would adopt a boy or a girl who had lost his or her family in the war. I thought of the young Orluks girl, the daughter of our neighbors on Pohulanka Street, and I already imagined her in our house in Lodz. That in itself was a sign of the peace of mind and an unexpected lack of anxiety that characterized us at the time. Despite what we were hearing, we thought ourselves personally immune.

One day, the count arrived and told us, "Mr. Chigryn has come to Sworotwa."

The news came out of the blue. All our peace vanished. We were shaken and expected complications because Chigryn looked 100 percent Jewish, and his accent was also very Jewish. Jan added that Mietek had asked for our address, but the count and the countess were absolutely against disclosing it to him. Jan told him only what we were doing but did not tell him where we were living. Mietek spent the first night with the Jewish family at the estate, and then Jan recommended him to one of the peasants in the nearby village, and that was where he was temporarily staying. "He will be better off where he is now than you are here," the count said. "I know these people."

We felt a little better because we could not help Mietek in any way, but our peace of mind vanished forever. It was only then that we began to understand how good our position in Burdakowszczyzna really was, despite all the hardships. Mietek told the count that the Krupowiczes did not want to keep him any longer and that he managed to find Sworotwa on foot, having walked for several days. We admired him for making it so far with his telling looks—without anyone stopping him along the way. A few days later, the count brought us the news that Mietek had left in the direction of Nowogrodek and that the peasant who was showing him the way had stolen his rucksack. We were depressed by this. Only when we found out that Mietek had made it to Nowogrodek did our hearts lighten a bit. The Jews over there would not let him die of hunger and cold, we thought.

Only after the war did we learn about his fate. From Nowogrodek he managed to get to Warsaw, to the ghetto, where he found his wife. Then he was seen in Bergen Belsen, where he died from blood poisoning following a tooth extraction.

After Mietek's appearance, we felt anxious, and we thanked God for every day that passed quietly and without bad news.

One day, we read from the Platers' faces that the news was bad. We were always pleased with their visits. They were our protectors, and we always tried to receive them the best we could. Since this time, the visit promised to be longer, Jan asked me to order for the horse to be unharnessed and fed. They came to tell us that Countess Halina had confided in the translator of the estate's "Sonderführer" (the special German administrator of agricultural estates). This translator was a Jew and now living in Horodyszcze. She had told him that we were Jewish as well, and she asked his advice. The translator supposedly said that Burdakowszczyzna was a very dangerous place for us because soon all the newcomers were going to be registered, and this registration was to be a means of filtering out the Jews hiding in the area. We, therefore, should immediately change our whereabouts. His suggestion was the following: Mother should go at once to Baranowicze to the Gebietskommissar's (the German regional administrator) office and ask there for work as a translator because she had heard that the position was vacant. Needless to say, Mother was not supposed to admit how she had found out about this. The idea surprised us by its impudence: this was walking straight into the lion's den.

The count and the countess had a different idea: we were supposed to find a place at another estate, one not in the immediate vicinity. One possibility was Huta, the place we had passed on our way from Wilno to Sworotwa. Of course we followed the Platers' advice and decided to look for a place elsewhere. Several days later, Mother set out for Huta. The little town was nearly one hundred kilometers from Burdakowszczyzna. After her departure, both my little sister and I felt very lonely. We loved Mother so much! We had gone through so many ordeals together, we had suffered together, we had risked our lives together, and we wanted her to be always with us. Our anxiety was well-founded: I was worried that someone might recognize Mother as Jewish, and I also wondered how she would cover such a distance. We were as if orphaned. I no longer washed myself; I slept in my clothes, impatient for Mother's return.

Mother came back after three days. We were as happy as if she had returned from a long journey to another continent. She recounted her trip to Huta and back. Both ways, she was fortunate to happen upon trucks that gave her a lift there and back. But the result of the trip was null. Huta had been taken over by the Belorussians, and the Poles were getting ready to leave. As her ostensible reason for looking for work, Mother gave our disinclination to be a burden to the Platers. We decided to try the other estates suggested by them. We sent my little sister to Sworotwa, and the two of us set out for an estate called Woroncza.

On our way there, we were supposed to stop at the Zubkowiczes' farm. We brought along some food—bread with pork fat—and marched onto a road we didn't know. We walked half a day without rest, through deep snow. At last, in some small woods, we stopped to rest and eat something. It was very cold. We were frozen to the bone. After a modest meal, we went on. Mother suffered from walking in her boots, which had a broken zipper. My feet, too, were snowy and heavy. In the afternoon, we reached the farm. We entered a clean, warm, nicely furnished room or hall. An elderly, distinguished gentleman with a gray goatee was playing solitaire. A mouth-watering smell of blintzes was wafting in from the kitchen.

Mr. Zubkowicz greeted us very coldly. "I have no room here. Let the count keep you at his place. I'm afraid that people will start talking if they notice you here, and they will suspect illegal activity—and I'm afraid of politics."

Mother looked offended, and she said in an ironic voice, "If you fear our presence here, we certainly won't remain here another moment; the count will find out how we were treated here." Mr. Zubkowicz was taken aback. Apparently he did not want his reputation in the count's eyes to suffer—Poles of that whole area respected Count Plater greatly. He began to smile and wanted to rectify what he had said, but we did not wait and flew out of there onto the road, leaving him with the impression that he had insulted poor aristocrats (Dunins).

It was the end of November. The days were short. When we left the Zubkowiczes', dusk began. The road turned, and we saw a village. We decided to spend the night there, and we asked a passer-by where the soltys's house was. The soltys was Polish (as was the whole village), and he received us very well as Poles. He found us good lodging with a young married couple. Our hosts were very kind to us. They seated us on benches, and we dined with them on dry potatoes and milk. Then they made us beds on wide, comfortable benches. It was warm. In the room next door, our hosts kissed passionately for many hours, and then sleep overcame them and us, too. It was still dark, and the moon was shining when everyone got up. The young hostess made the fire, while I went outside to get the water. It was so quiet outside, and it seemed so safe that I thought with great envy about the happiness of these people who did not have to escape to save their lives, who had no anxieties and could live through the war here. In the meantime, the hostess heated up some pork fat in a pan and began frying blintzes made with flour and potatoes. They were delicious, and we could eat as much fat as we wanted. We ate our fill and were ready for the road. Our hosts showed us how we should proceed and told us that the lords of Woroncza were excellent people.

It was light when we set out. The sun was rising, and the snow was sparkling like diamonds. We passed through a village. White smoke rose from the chimneys. "They're probably frying blintzes," I thought to myself. The windowpanes reflected the sun, which blinded us. A thick, fluffy layer of snow covered all the buildings. When we walked it squeaked pleasantly under our feet. We arrived at a crossroads and did not know which way to go. We chose the road on the left. We were far away when I looked back and noticed a man at the crossroads. I ran back, and halfway to him, I shouted, "Which is the way to Woroncza?" It turned out that we had gone the wrong way. I called Mother, and soon we were on the road leading directly to the estate. There was still one and a half kilometers to walk. We saw the large Woroncza forest, and, as we approached, we distinguished the estate buildings. We were very glad because we hoped that they would take us in. The place appeared safe; it was so far off the road, and it seemed that there was no lack of food.

We entered the palace through a large hallway. It was nice and warm inside, and we were greeted with smiles and asked to take our coats off. I threw my jacket off with joy, and I radiated warmth and contentment. Mother introduced herself and gave them the letter from the countess. Our hosts' smiles became even warmer after they read the letter. First of all, they served us a delicious meal. We did not eat too much because we had decided not to seem greedy so that they would take us in all the more willingly. Then came the questions: which Dunins are you from, the Borkowski or the Wasowicz? Mother replied that we are from the Borkowski branch. "Oh, so you must know Mrs. X, or perhaps you're related to her?" Mother replied that the Dunin family was large and that she did not know the lady in question.

"The letter from Mrs. Halina was quite unnecessary. After all, one can recognize a lord by his boots," said Mrs. Czarnecka.

Mother smiled at this triumph. Suddenly, a pretty young woman entered the room. "Countess Przedzielska," Mrs. Czarnecka introduced her. That was when I thought that I would be as happy as in paradise in this place—I would even have a girlfriend! The conversation moved in the right direction. We were asked why we had to leave the Burdakowszczyzna estate. We explained that registration was going to take place there that had as its aim the sifting out of the Polish refugees and that that could prove fatal to those who were discovered. They were surprised that the Platers could not accommodate us at their place, and we attributed that to the economic and housing situation there. "Here, too, we are overcrowded," they said, "and despite our best intentions, we cannot accommodate yet another family." We tried to persuade them by saying that we would not be in the way and would work. They talked among themselves for a moment, and it seemed that they had decided to let us stay in the farmhands' living quarters, but then they changed their minds, and the son, Mr. Czarnowski, asked us whether we would like to get to Warsaw.

We were shocked. We had no idea that going to Warsaw was a possibility, and that was why we never considered it. After a moment's consideration, Mother agreed to this suggestion. It turned out that an acquaintance of the young Czarnowski was a translator in one of the main offices in Baranowicze, and he could "organize" passes for us. "If he can't get you a pass, nobody can," said Czarnowski. "He is a kind person and will help you in all your troubles." Then he wrote a warm letter to this acquaintance, a Mr. Miecznikowski, which we were to hand to him when we would see him in Baranowicze.

Our visit in Woroncza was coming to an end. We were already imagining the hard road home on foot. It was not exactly a pleasure to walk in deep snow through fields, woods, and villages. So when Mrs. Czarnecka had the horses harnessed to a large, comfortable sleigh that would take us directly to Sworotwa, we breathed with relief. We bid them a heartfelt farewell and got on the road. The horses pulled swiftly, and the sleigh glided easily on the hardened snow. Branches and bushes passed by, and now and then we received a load of snow falling from a tree. We were unspeakably happy. There were moments when we truly believed that we were the Count and the Countess Dunin. A few kilometers before Sworotwa, we began to freeze, and that was why we got off the sleigh eagerly when we arrived there. We walked into the house at once and were immediately greeted by Halina. Mother told her quickly that we were going to Warsaw, and the countess passed the news to her husband right away: "Mrs. Dunin is leaving for Warsaw."

In Baranowicze we were going to stay with the brother of the peasant with whom we had lived in Andrzejowicze. We went by wagon and not by sleigh because there was a thaw. We arrived in Baranowicze at the time when the ghetto was being organized there. The Jews were bringing all their belongings to a part of the town surrounded with barbed wire. They walked in the streets with the patches in front and in back. Some were elegantly dressed and carried briefcases—those were most likely the employees of the Judenrat (Jewish administration appointed by the Germans). They made an odd impression, as they walked fast with a preoccupied look. In front of the Gebietskommissariat (German regional administration), there were many Jewish workers. One of them, with hands red from the cold and the same preoccupied expression on his face, was carrying a pile of clean laundry. He walked with quick, short steps. Germans walked about with their long whips and "kept order."

Before going to Miecznikowski's, I stopped at a barber's; my hair had not been cut in months, and I had a shaggy head. Several Germans sitting at the barber's were discussing the entrance of the USA into the war. It was clear that they were not thrilled by the news. Suddenly, loud screams resounded in the street. The barber looked through the window and then said, laughing, "That's good. A German beat up a Jew."

We had to take a roundabout way to get to Miecznikowski's apartment. All the streets that led there directly were blocked with barbed wire surrounding the ghetto. Mr. Miecznikowski promised to obtain the passes for us and offered that we could stay with him until that time. We accepted happily because there was no room at the peasant's where we had arrived. In the end, I stayed at Mr. Miecznikowski's, and Mother, with my little sister, remained at the brother of the "American." It was not easy to obtain the pass. The Germans had stopped issuing them and made no exceptions. Every day, Mr. Miecznikowski returned from the city with bad news, and at last he said that it was impossible to get the passes.

Our situation was not a happy one. We were as if suspended in mid-air, with no place to live and no means of earning a livelihood. The departure for Warsaw was but a dream. The peasants with whom Mother and my little sister were staying began to show their discontent with the prolonged visit. The lack of basic conveniences and of warm food had a depressing effect on us as well. We didn't know what to do with ourselves, what to do period. Then we remembered the advice of the Jewish translator, who had suggested when we were still in Sworotwa that we ought to go to the Gebietskommissariat to apply for the post of translator in Horodyszcze.

It was difficult to decide to walk straight in the lion's den, as it were, but our situation encouraged us, and Mother, having thought out every word she was going to use, went to the office of the "supermen." Judging by Mother's expression when she came home, our matters were in a good way. The very fact that she came back confirmed it. The person who received her was the vice-Gebietskommissar Wolf. Without any difficulty, he agreed at once to hire Mother as the "Dolmetscher von Rayon Verwaltung" (translator in the regional management). Wolf wrote a letter to the mayor telling him to employ Mother and to take care of us! We had never expected the latter. It was an important trump card for us. We were to leave the following day after dinner. Seated in the wagon that had been officially assigned to us, we felt very secure. We felt immune from all danger. The road was interminably long. We were daydreaming about our future life in Horodyszcze.

We arrived at the village Nowosiolki, where they were supposed to give us fresh horses. As it was already dark, we had to spend the night in the village. The village administrator sent us to a family that was going to put us up. They were an older couple. They told us how anxious they were about the near future: "When they have killed all the Jews, they might also kill us." This was less than a month after the great massacre of the Jews of Horodyszcze. They remembered that day with terror because "if they can do it with them, they can do the same to us." The peasant's wife told us that she had talked to the Germans about that, and they had reassured her by saying, "Don't be afraid. We are killing only the Jews. You can go on living in peace." She, however, didn't trust their words and kept asking every few minutes, "Will they kill us?" We answered, "God only knows," and we sighed. *Don't let them be so calm,* we thought to ourselves. The following morning, we were already on the uneven, bumpy road to Horodyszcze. We felt a bit ill at ease.

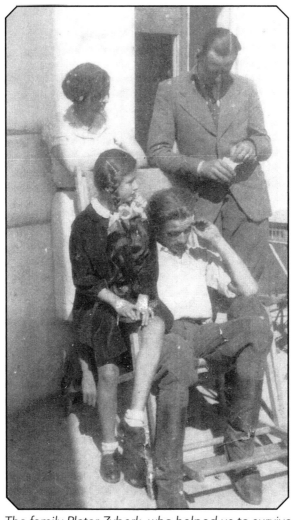

The family Plater-Zyberk, who helped us to survive
Upper left: Halina Plater-Zyberk
Upper right: Jan Plater-Zyberk
Lower left: Roza, their daughter
Lower right: Wyszek, brother of Jan
Date: Soon after liberation

Halina and Jan Plater-Zyberk
Sopot, Poland
Date unknown

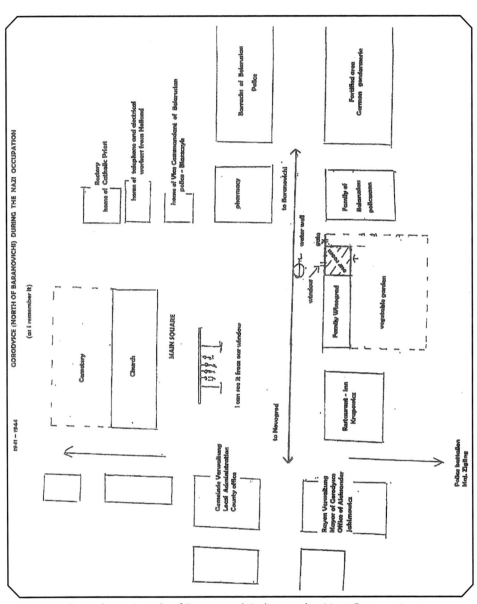

Gorodysce (north of Baranovichi) during the Nazi Occupation
1941–1944
Map by George Dynin

CHAPTER FIVE

WE RODE INTO THE city with a sense of surrendering ourselves into enemy hands. The wagon stopped next to a large wooden building. "The Reyonova Uprava (regional administration) is here," said our peasant and motioned to the building. Mother got off the wagon and entered the building. My little sister and I took our things off the wagon, and we waited for Mother's return with great impatience. We didn't have to wait long. Mother returned with a spry and energetic step; it was clear that she had taken on her new role. The mayor asked the chief district administrator to find lodgings for us. Our things had to remain for the time being at the "Reyonova Uprava." Many clerks were employed there. We stood in the hallway and could observe the figures passing by us. One of the clerks who worked there was a translator with a yellow patch. The Germans must have wanted to replace her with an "Aryan force," since they had announced her post as vacant.

Our new accommodations were a room in a large wooden house, similar to other houses in the town. I was heavily depressed by the conviction that the house had belonged to people who were murdered. I didn't even want to sit down in a chair because it was a remnant of the "killed ones." I was loath to touch any of the furniture in the room because it was, in my mind, saturated with the blood of innocent people. All the furniture consisted of two chairs, a wobbly table, a couch with many exposed springs, and a camp-bed. It was very cold. Our neighbor gave us some wood, and that was what we used to cook our first soup in Horodyszcze. The room remained chilly because the house had not been heated in a long time. The sun had long set, and the little smoky lamp gave only a tiny flame, which was our only light. Mother spread a clean sheet over the dirty, torn couch and then piled up our comforters and all the warm clothes that we had so that we wouldn't be cold at night. I was in despair, fighting with myself so as not to lie down on the couch left behind by the dead. I decided to spend the night sitting in a chair. In the meantime Mother and my little sister slipped under the covers, and Dzidzia exclaimed joyously because of the blissful warmth. I, on the other hand, was trembling with cold. Fatigue and the cold conquered my scruples, and a moment later I was lying down with the comforter pulled all the way to my nose. It felt good and warm.

In our first days there, Horodyszcze made a terrible impression on us. In several parts of town, there were storage places with things left "after the Jews." The peasants from nearby villages came in a throng to "seize" some rags. The chief district administrator and the forester were the main organizers of the sale of these things. They were both wearing leather jackets and, in their leather chauffeur caps with fat faces, looked like two demons. To make things worse, the forester would break out in satanic laughter every couple of minutes. He spoke Belorussian to everyone, even though he was Polish, and his laughter could be heard for miles. Those two were at the top of the pyramid of people who fed on human blood. They were living it up, literally drowning in gold. A peasant could not buy anything without the chief district administrator's permission, and, to get the permission, he had to pay a bribe. One of the storage places was near our house, and I could see how the peasants literally fought over every scrap. We told ourselves that we would not remain long in this blood-tainted place. After all, we had spent a month here, a month there, so now, too, we wouldn't linger in this town. But subconsciously, we knew that we would stay here for a long time.

Our room was always semi-dark because the window pane was

broken and had been patched with newspapers. The only source of light was the glass door that at night was closed off with wooden shutters. Then we felt as if we were safer and cozier. The chief administrator gave us a sack of buckwheat and oats. We knew that those grains had to come from a Jewish household, but not having another option, we accepted them. The chief administrator was surprised that we were not showing up to get "some things." Mother answered that, for now, we had enough of our own and that as soon as we needed something, we would come to him.

As with all the civil servants in the region, Mother had the right to some firewood—but the wood was wet and of the worst quality. I had a very hard time separating the roughly hewn logs. It took me several hours to get enough wood to prepare a meal. Here, veritable tortures of Tantalus would begin. The wet wood would not burn. I had to blow out the entire capacity of my lungs, and even before the fire would truly burn, I was utterly exhausted. During the cooking, one of us had to watch it all the time for fear that the treasure—fire—did not become extinguished. When the soup began to cook, we would jump for joy— that was how hungry and tired we were from the effort of making the fire. Our joy came from the fact that a few minutes later, we would be able to fill our stomachs with a hot meal. All in all, we went hungry most of the time. The bread that was rationed was not enough. We spent all our free time waiting for food.

Our first acquaintance in Horodyszcze was Dr. Piaskowski, the regional doctor. He feigned openness with my mother and criticized many in the town. He pretended to be a Polish patriot and prophesized a fast defeat of the Germans. Piaskowski invited us to dinner, and we eagerly accepted. It had been a long time since we had eaten such delicacies as at that dinner and since we had drunk tea with sugar.

Piaskowski had a wife and two small boys. The wife was a pharmacist, and she ran the local pharmacy. The kids looked very ordinary and had terrible manners. The doctor criticized various pre-war characters as well and told us many stories from those times. He was very talkative and, at the time, we thought him interesting. He laughed at the Soviet rule and recounted his "heroic deeds for the good of society." We learned later that during the Soviet rule, he had occupied an important post and pretended to be a communist. His wife, who, we found out later, was a Jew pretending to be a Pole, said to us right away, "As soon as you arrived we thought you were German or Jewish." In reply we just laughed. "How exactly did you get a job here?" asked Mrs. Piaskowska.

"I was sent by Wolf, the vice-Gebietskommissar," replied Mother. We could see from their faces that the doctor and his wife were a bit confounded by that answer. Soon afterward, the doctor began to assure us about his gratitude to the Germans for having liberated them from the Bolsheviks. Then he quickly blended the concept of the Bolshevik with that of a peasant and claimed that he hated them all. He squeezed everything he could out of his patients who were peasants—their entire property. He explained that he had no scruples in charging peasants so much because peasants were thieves and swindlers.

When the doctor found out that I had finished the penultimate grade in middle school, he offered me the position of tutor to his two boys, in return for board and some money. I decided to try this job as a teacher-tutor. When the time came for my first lesson, I had no idea how I should begin. I deemed it best to start with drawing. I began to draw a car and then a ship, trying to convince my pupils to imitate me. There was no question of that. They were real rascals. They began to fight at once, at first with bare hands and then with raw sausages they got from the kitchen. Needless to say, the sausages broke and the contents landed on the floor. I tried to calm them down the best I could. At that point Mrs. Piaskowska came home. When she saw the raging battle and, most importantly, the broken sausages, she threw me an angry glance and said, "You have caused me great damages." I began to make excuses without feeling guilty in the least. A moment later her husband arrived, and when he found out what was going on, he screamed that all guests were crooks. I became red in the face and left their house quite offended.

At home, we talked about how Mrs. Piaskowska had told us about her acquaintance with the German gendarme Reines. Mother knew this German from his "visits" at the regional office. Whenever he ran into Mother in the street, he always greeted her politely. Reines received pork fat from the Piaskowskis, which he claimed to be sending to his family in Germany. He was a frequent guest at their house, and they always received him generously in order to get into his good graces. Reines claimed that he had been sent to the area to clear it of Jews and of communists. We wondered whether he meant catching the Jews who were hiding as "Aryans" or the killing of the few remaining victims in the ghetto. We stopped seeing the Piaskowskis and began to regret that we had ever gotten to know them.

Mother's work in the office went slowly at first. Without any previous practice, she had to translate documents from German into Belorussian and vice-versa. But with the passage of time, her translations improved. In a short time, she was able to gain the approval of all her coworkers. Her greatest enemy, the secretary, also became her friend. Because of our protection from the Gebietskommissar, even the mayor acted decently toward us.

On the second Sunday after our arrival in Horodyszcze, we decided to visit the church. Having been taught by the countess how to behave, we went to the morning Mass. It would have looked suspicious to everyone if we did not go to church on a Sunday. The day was windy and cold. We entered the entryway to the church, and from there we walked inside. I wanted to be with Mother, and, therefore, I followed her. Only after a while did I realize that men were standing separately on the right, and halfway through my false step, I wanted to turn back. But, at that very moment, I realized that someone could notice that, and so I finished making my step and looked with concentration at the large painting of Christ hanging above the altar, as if that had been the aim of my forward step. Having stood there for a moment, I delicately backed away into the part for men. A little later, I realized that we had committed other errors as well. Each person entering the church crossed himself or herself, while we did not. That was a terrible mistake, because people in the church paid attention to each new arrival. From where I was standing, I could see Mother. She was wearing the only coat she had, a black summer one, and she seemed a bit stooped; in my opinion, she looked like a Jewess. As a new face in the church, she attracted the attention of the women around her. They devoured her with their eyes. I felt very odd. I was simply afraid that they might recognize her as Jewish.

It was terribly cold in the church, and I was slowly freezing to the bone. I clenched my teeth in order to make it to the end. We had to kneel down several times during the service. When I saw others kneeling down, I followed their example. When they beat their breast and whispered something, I imitated them and whispered random words to create the impression that I was "one of the herd." I noticed that Mrs. Piaskowska was in the church as well. I saw that she opened her lips wide when she prayed. Her whispered prayers were loud and resounded throughout much of the church. The doctor's wife even took Holy Communion. At last the Mass was over, and the priest blessed the congregation. We could go outside and return home where a hot meal was waiting for us. I met with Mother by the door. She was almost paralyzed with the cold. She could barely walk. We only revived once we reached the house. It wasn't very warm there, but we didn't have to watch our every movement—we were free. Mother told me that she felt observed by everyone and that they must have suspected something. I made light of her fears without being convinced, however, that that was not the case. I did not want to put Mother in a bad mood.

Daily difficulties with obtaining firewood, daily pulling up of water from the iced well, the monotony of the food, the lack of good news, the cramped living conditions in our little room, as well as Mother's difficulties at her job in the office—all this made our life seem hard. Mother was in a particularly risky position because she was at all times surrounded by people who spoke about a variety of topics. She had to be on her guard not to betray her Jewishness with a careless word. She even made mistakes on purpose in German because it was well-known that the Jews had a gift for languages and spoke German impeccably.

Mayor Aleksander Jakimowicz was the master of life and death in

Horodyszcze. Everyone feared him, and everyone removed their hats from their heads at the mere sight of him. His permanent residence was in Lodz—that was where his wife and child, as well as a sister-in-law, were living. He was a tall, handsome man with black hair. He had a nice voice and at first made a good impression. He claimed that his family came from the town of Glebokie in Belarus, and that was how he justified his Belorussian nationality. During the war with the Soviets, he was in Germany, working at a farm. The moment the Belorussian committee was formed, he joined it and was placed in his current position. Every few days, the mayor went to Baranowicze. He wrote reports that he did not give Mother to translate. One of the mayor's duties was to gather denunciations. When a peasant would come with a denunciation, the mayor would lock himself up with the peasant in his office, in the presence of the vice-mayor Laciszonek, and prepare a report.

The Gremjak family was well-represented in all the local offices. Andrei was the treasurer; his brother Volodya had a lesser, somewhat fictitious post in the office, because in reality he was the mayor's "aide-de-camp." It was said that he participated actively in the expulsion of the Jews from their homes. Their father, always drunk, pretended to the post of the judge in the "court" that was being formed.

Mother worked in the same room with a typist, Janka Pietraszycka, and the two became good friends. Janka hated the Germans with all her heart, and she felt the same way about all their devoted collaborators, beginning with the mayor himself. She had a lot of compassion for the Jews and said that her father, who was taken away by the Soviets, had regular commercial dealings with the Jews. Naturally, Mother never told her about our origins.

One day, a German by the name of Bertram arrived from the Gebietskommissariat for an inspection of the Jewish workshops, the so-called "artels." Mother had to go there with him and with the mayor to serve as a translator if need be. During the inspection of a tailor's artel, the German looked underneath a pillow on a bed and found a piece of fabric there. He looked at his victim—the tailor—with a triumphant grimace: "Where did you get that, you cursed fool!" he screamed. The miserable man, paralyzed by fear, could not utter a word, and that rendered the Kraut even more certain that he had caught a "criminal" who wanted to sew something on the sly, that is, pocketing the earned money himself instead of depositing it in the artel account, i.e., for the Germans. Who knows what would have happened to the slave if the artel manager, a Pole, had not explained that the fabric was "legal." After the finished work, the mayor invited the German to dinner.

Christmas came. We gratefully accepted the Platers' invitation to join them for the holidays. It was of double benefit to us: first of all, because it "advertised" our good relations with the Platers and, secondly, if we were to stay at home, we would have to prepare for the holidays ourselves so that our neighbors would not think it strange that we did not serve Christmas dishes—and Mother had no clue as to what one cooked for Christmas. Soon, the entire office knew that "the translator was invited for Christmas to Sworotwa." This was Mother's doing; she spread the news quite purposefully.

The few days spent in Sworotwa allowed us an incredible rest of our nerves. We felt much more carefree with the Platers than in Horodyszcze, despite the fact that Stefan, one of the three youths who had arrived two months earlier, was still with them. He turned out to be a very amiable young man. He respected my mother immensely and was very candid with me. He told us, laughing, about the count and countess's daily "menu." Unwilling to improve their diet at the expense of somebody else's estate, they covered up hunger by drinking buttermilk. Fortunately, he said, for the holidays Mr. Plater's brother had sent some meat and other food from Swojatycze. We forgot about all the evil we had seen and heard in Horodyszcze, about our narrow, dark, and cold room, about the wet firewood, and about having to pull the water out of the iced well, where one had to tie and untie the tangled bucket chain in the frost.

Christmas went by quickly, and we returned to Horodyszcze with heavy hearts. Hopelessness entered our souls. Our good mood went to the dogs when, having crossed the threshold of our chilly room, we beheld our bed of misery—the couch with protruding broken springs. February let itself be felt with strong frost. Water left in a bowl froze. There was no hope of any improvement on the front. The Germans were fighting near Leningrad, and their local orders indicated that they were there to stay for a good long time, perhaps for good. Our moods were heavy, and our life was heavy as well.

One day, Mother came home from the office before noon, which normally did not happen. She said, "Things are not good. The secretary told me that gendarme Reines had whispered to the mayor that the lieutenant from the Gebietskommissariat had passed on a confidential message that in the Rayon-Verwaltung there was a Jewish translator working under a false last name." Mother told me all this quickly, in the same manner in which the secretary had told it to her, and it seemed that he himself did not give the matter much import. Mother also feigned indifference and continued to work "calmly." This time, I didn't even know how to console my mother. I kissed her good-bye, and she returned to the office to continue her heroic performance.

In a moment, I realized various facts: namely that we did not appreciate how good we had had it thus far, as well as that we had no possibility of escape now, in the winter, and that, practically speaking, we were lost, although the latter realization refused to fit in my mind. I felt like a man in prison who has been sentenced to death, but who, for now, is still enjoying every passing moment of life. I suddenly realized the beauty of the world in its external form and the weight of the fact that I was losing this world, that I would not see it again. My thoughts were running in all directions. It was total chaos. I tried to convince myself that I was not in the world, that I had never existed, that my life was another man's dream. At that very moment, my little sister's voice awoke the consciousness of being alive, and the subconscious of every living being revived my will to live. *How shall I save myself? How? Who can give me an answer? Who was to give me advice?*

We were in a hopeless situation, at the mercy of an enemy who wanted to destroy us. I leaned against the door and observed the goings-on in the town. Oh, how I envied them! I would have given everything to be able to switch places with them. *Oh, how happy they are, and they don't understand or feel it! Why is it like this?* I could not find an answer, so I simply chased away the questions: *how to escape? how to survive?* There was no answer. Nonetheless, I conquered the fear that was convincing me we were lost. That moment was very brief; later I did not think about it. I defined our situation as hopeless, but I did not allow the thought of imminent death close to me. I was somewhere on the border between life and death. In the window repaired with newspaper, there was only one crack through which one could look outside. I walked up to it without thinking. Through the crack I could see the church tower.

My sister enjoying the swans on a small lake

My parents at the Berlin Zoo
Date unknown

These two photos were with us during the Holocaust. Not only
did they remind us of good times, but they also were shown
everywhere by us as "proof" of our "Aryan background."

CHAPTER SIX

(Note: The following passage describes the worst time of my life, and, therefore, I wrote it as though it were happening to someone else.)

HE FELT WARM, AND at the same time, a strange shiver ran through him: "This will save us," he said.

He said it forcefully, and his facial expression changed. He felt very strong now. "We shall survive. We shall survive," he repeated. An unknown force was filling his entire being. He looked once again through the window, then knelt down and began to pray. It was a never-ending prayer. God awoke in him. He was in a mode in which he was controlled by an order. *"Now you must go to the church,"* said the voice. He quickly combated his unwillingness to go to the empty, cold church. He knew that someone was directing him: the One who would save him.

He entered the church through the narrow, open doors. He was one-on-one with God. Something told him to approach the altar. He knelt down and continued to pray. He didn't want to lean on the barrier of the altar: "Let me be uncomfortable," he said, and that is how his expiation began. His knees were hurting him from kneeling on the stony, cold floor while he extended his arms toward the altar and begged for grace. Oh, how he would have liked to cry; what a relief that would bring! He tried to cry; he could not, so he continued to pray. He was utterly close to God. He had given himself over into God's authority. Leaving the church, he smiled an unearthly smile. He was not afraid of anything or anyone.

At home, he made a fire and put on the soup. Pleasant warmth permeated the room. It was only a moment of relaxation because soon, Mother came from work. She was devastated and could barely stand up. She brought along a feeling of helplessness and despair. She told him once again about what the secretary had said. She had begun to see little signs that the mayor was taking Reines's claim seriously.

"There are no two ways about it; things are not good," she said. "Why didn't we go to the ghetto in Wilno? There, we would have had a chance, while here we are sure to perish."

He began to let his mother influence him, but, unlike her, he was not in extreme despair. They ate the soup.

"As long as one lives, one must eat," said his mother.

They were longing for sleep that would transport them from reality into nothingness or into fantasy. They thought that they would not give up those hours of sleep for anything in the world. They had not appreciated them ever before. *Sleep* is paradise. Falling asleep, they no longer saw the fat face of the little stocky gendarme Reines, or the mayor, or his secretary, or Horodyszcze. Their fears and worries ceased to exist. Good sleep had them in its keeping. The awakening was very rude. Reality was in front of them with all its evil.

"When you see that I've been arrested, you both run away. There is nothing to lose anyway," said Mother.

He grew cold at these words, but did not wish to say good-bye in such hopelessness. "You'll see that this will pass," he said.

Mother was touched, and she kissed him, saying, "You really think so, Son?"

He was extremely anxious. He wanted to reestablish a balance of spirit through prayer. After kneeling a long time and reciting various prayers as penance, he felt reassured. Nonetheless, he counted every minute that separated him from his mother's return from the office. He greeted his mother as if he had not seen her in years. He wished to calm her down at all cost. Above all, he was eager to show her that he was not afraid, so he began by telling her which soup he had made and what he'd put into it. Mother soon recounted her impressions from the office and drew the conclusion that the mayor didn't trust her. The worst piece of news, however, was the mayor's trip to Baranowicze.

"I'm sure he's going there because of me," she said. They discussed the possibility of bribing the mayor. They had no money, but several beautiful pieces of jewelry from before the war were still in their possession. Mother was already rehearsing the likely speech she would have to make while handing him the jewels. His soul was sick, and the feeling of hopelessness was taking him over. He moved like an automaton. He would have gladly remained idle, but they needed water to live, and fire as well.

He referred to himself then as a "living corpse." He awaited the mayor's arrival with terror. It would be a miracle if, after his arrival, everything would continue as usual, they thought.

Soon the good night came, filled with strange dreams. Mother dreamed of her father, who was chasing away wild beasts that were trying to devour her.

Again, the awakening brought about its reality. The day went on seemingly as usual. Mother went to the office, while Jurek began to do things around the house. During those nerve-wracking days, their faces had changed—their cheeks had sunk, and their noses were longer. That was not good, because now they resembled the local Jews. Jurek was very conscious of that, and it tormented him. In the mornings, he prayed as usual, and that helped him regain some balance, but Mother's arrival from the office depressed him because she brought along with her the air of pessimism and hopelessness.

That morning, he went to get water as always. When a woman passed him with two empty buckets, he thought it a bad omen. Next to the well, there stood a group of people. Jurek tried to avoid their glances because he felt that fear looked out of his eyes, and that therefore he resembled a Jew. He heard clearly that someone in that group said "a Jew," and he could feel the people's eyes on him. His heart was beating loudly, and he felt weak. He barely pulled up a bucket of water and dragged it home, accompanied by the glances of strangers. He felt the same way as when he had heard about Reines's "confidential news" from Mother. But he did not share his experience with his mother or his little sister when Mother came from the office.

After his return from Baranowicze, the mayor's attitude toward Mother did not seem changed. Jurek picked that up as a leitmotif as he tried to reassure his mother. "Perhaps God will have mercy on us and will save us," said Mother.

It was not late, perhaps six o'clock, when they heard steps approaching their apartment. They trembled unwittingly. The steps came closer, and soon someone was knocking on the shutters. Mother asked, "Who is it?" It was Volodya, the mayor's "aide-de-camp." He said that the mayor was asking Mother to come to him at once in an important matter. Volodya added that Laciszonek, the vice mayor, was there as well. He left, leaving them in a terrible state.

"The fact that Laciszonek is there is proof that they want to write up a report," said Mother. "The mayor always takes a witness in such cases," she added. The fact that it was evening convinced them even more that their fate was being decided.

Jurek understood well that he himself was the tangible proof that would decide about their life or death. *This cursed tradition made our misery,* he thought. He knew that the enemy could prove very quickly that he was Jewish, and thereby destroy his mother and his sister. The only hope was in God's hands. When Mother left, he fell to his knees and prayed fervently. Mother did not return for a long time, while he continued to kneel and pray. He did not budge, and his legs were quite numb. At times he felt pain, then a sensation of cold spread throughout his whole body, and sometimes he did not feel his legs at all. Mother was still not back.

Two hours later, he heard her steps from afar. When she was climbing the steps, he opened the door for her with a smile. The matter for which she had been called to the office was professional; she had been needed to translate a new German "announcement" (directive) that was to be made public in the morning. Jurek thanked God in his thoughts.

That moment marked a great divide in the family's feelings. They began to trust that there was a chance of survival—a spark of hope burned in their minds. The first wave of danger receded, making visible various thoughts that compelled them to act—thoughts that had previously been drowned in the depths of terror.

The sleep was strong and healthy, and the awakening was not as terrible as before. When Mother came back from the office, we began to discuss our situation. I was the most serious and convincing proof of our Semitic origin. There was no question that to save us, I had to separate myself from my mother and sister. We decided that I would go to Swojatycze, the estate managed by Jan Plater's brother. We remembered that his brother, Wyszek, was supposed to travel to Warsaw at about that time; that was what the Platers had told us in Sworotwa. Mother was hoping that Wyszek would take me with him. To encourage him, we wanted to give him one of our remaining jewels, a beautiful diamond butterfly. Swojatycze was a few dozen kilometers away. Mother knew that, from time to time, the manager of another estate located six kilometers from Swojatycze came to the Rayonova Uprava. The only thing was not to miss that chance.

On a frosty February day, the manager did come, and after a short conversation with Mother, he willingly agreed to give me a lift to his estate. The weather was sunny that day. The frost was extreme. Red stripes appeared in the sky, and people were saying that that meant war. Hearing this made us feel better. I dreamed of being in the harshest possible front conditions—just so as not to be in the power of Hitler. My mood improved.

"The signs in the sky are good omens," I said to Mother, and already, in front of my eyes, I saw the scene of liberation. Saying good-bye to

Mother was hard. I realized that I was leaving her in great danger, but I did not, even for a moment, entertain the thought that I might not see her again, which, after all, was quite possible.

The sleigh moved fast. The weather was spectacular. The reflections of the sun in the snow resembled sparkly diamonds; many traces of animals marked the surface of the snow on both sides of the road, and the bells adorning the bridle chimed in the rhythm of the horse's trot. All this was so wonderful that, willy-nilly, I forgot the aim and the reason for my trip. Three of us rode along: the estate manager, his secretary, and I. The manager was a merry man, and he knew Wyszek from Swojatycze very well indeed.

As the ostensible goal of my journey, I said that I was looking for a better job. Our conversation was suddenly interrupted when we saw a fox approaching the sleigh from the road. I was amazed that such a flighty animal did not show any signs of fear and, on the contrary, was coming up close to us. The manager explained that foxes are very fond of the sound of bells and that they direct themselves toward that sound. We rode up about twenty-five meters from the fox and stopped. The fox did not move and then slowly, spurred by the shouts of our little group, returned to the woods. Farther on our journey, we passed various villages and a great forest. The cold was beginning to bother me. My thin jacket was not enough for a heavy frost. The sun was setting. My legs became numb. I had to get out of the sleigh and run around a bit.

"Only fifteen kilometers to go!" the manager encouraged us. It was becoming unbearably cold. In front of us, there was a limitless plain, cut through in the middle by a path made by the traveling sleighs. Somewhere in the distance, we could see some buildings. "From there it's as close as if one were to reach with a hand," the manager pointed to the distant buildings.

I clenched my teeth. I had to withstand it. My thoughts were taking fantastic shapes, and I was overcome by an irresistible desire to sleep. But I knew that at this moment sleep was my enemy. I bit my lips in order not to lose consciousness, but I sobered up completely when the manager said, "Well, here we are!"

I jumped out of the sleigh and suddenly felt very well. In a single moment, I forgot about all I had suffered on the road. The closeness of my goal put me back on my feet, but it also reminded me about the reason of my escapade. Ahead of me there were six more kilometers to cross on foot. I thanked the manager for the ride and for the offer of spending the night, and I set out following the route that he had indicated. I felt very confident and was in a decent mood, despite the fact that I was very hungry. The cold wind penetrated my thin jacket. I walked fast, not paying attention to the figures who passed me by. The world was becoming gray. I could distinguish the manor buildings. I didn't ask anyone for directions. I guessed that the buildings belonged to Swojatycze. It was already dark when I reached the park, where there stood a large palace that clearly had seen better times. I slowed down and looked around. I had arrived, and I wanted to extend the moment of arrival, paid for by such a hard road. I felt that a new stage of my struggle for life was beginning at this moment. I quickly found the path leading to the front door, and I stood before it momentarily.

A woman opened the door, probably the housekeeper. When I learned that Wyszek was not at home and was in Baranowicze, I felt a bit awkward. But I had no choice; I had to wait for him. Wyszek arrived late at night. He greeted me very warmly. I explained briefly the reasons for my arrival. It was very difficult to obtain a pass to go to Warsaw, and as Wyszek was himself trying to get one, he had a clear picture of the situation. It was with difficulty that I managed to say something about paying him: "You'll have a souvenir from us."

Wyszek replied that he did not wish to rescue people for money, although, on the other hand, he was not a charitable institution, that is, he could not sacrifice his time, effort, and money for someone for nothing. He seemed to be suggesting that he could not help me. But, in the end, he did not let me convince him for too long and gave in to my entreaties. He did say that if his parents knew that he was rescuing people for money, they would disown him. A few days later, Wyszek was supposed to go to Baranowicze again. It was there that he would try in every conceivable way to obtain a pass for me. All the while, I would remain at the estate. The uncertainty of the situation, combined with the fear for the safety of my mother and my little sister, depressed me considerably. Wyszek showed me pictures and told me about his life, and that filled my time a little. He treated me as if I were a good friend.

We discussed various political and social issues. He held a characteristic point of view on the peasant question. The peasant would always remain the enemy of the lord, because he would be content with his fate only once he had achieved the same standard of life as his master. And that, naturally, would never happen. From the photographs I gathered that, in "the good old times," he did much horseback riding and that the estate was always full of guests and residents.

Two days passed, and Wyszek went to Baranowicze. I was left alone with the empty walls of the palace and the witch-like housekeeper. The housekeeper was extremely devoted to the "young master," and that showed in the way she was feeding me. Apparently she wanted to save a little at the expense of my stomach. Cold and hunger tormented me during Wyszek's entire absence. To keep myself busy, I chopped wood and arranged it in a woodshed. The weather was sunny. The sunset was red, and the air was dry and frosty.

Sometimes when I was left alone in the palace, I thought of God and called for His help. I understood that my situation was hopeless without God's help. Those prayers gave me strength to survive the difficult moments.

Wyszek arrived in the evening of the third day. "Unfortunately, I was not able to obtain a pass for you," was his answer.

Oddly enough, I did not feel too concerned by this. I missed Mother terribly, although, at the same time, I feared the return to the "lion's den." In my mind's eye, I saw various scenes of destruction of my family by the enemy. It occurred to me for a moment that perhaps my mother and my sister were no more and that I would return directly for my execution. Nonetheless, I had no doubts about whether to return. My yearning to see them took the upper hand over all feelings of fear and uncertainty. Oh, how I wished to be already next to Mother, to be able to console her, to give her courage! *If I arrive and everything is all right, that means that the worst is behind us,* I thought. So, in the end, Wyszek's answer was perhaps to my liking. I still let him know, however, that I wanted to get to Warsaw at all cost, because, in truth, I couldn't tell if that wasn't my last chance for survival. In the morning, I was to leave to go back. Wyszek gave me the sleigh from the estate.

And again, the road through the white plains, the woods, and the frost biting to the bone. Every few minutes, I jumped out of the sleigh and ran around a little to warm up. The peasant riding with me did the same. I consoled myself with the fact that the distance was diminishing. The frost was so bad that I was not sure I would make it alive. I ran by the sleigh more than I rode in it because, after a few minutes of riding, my legs were like logs. I lost count of time and space. I woke as if from sleep when we were already close to Horodyszcze. I was terrified. I began to pray and call for God's help. A small red bird flew across the road and sat on a nearby tree. I took it to be a good omen, and I entered the hateful town almost calmly. Mother was still at work. I greeted my little sister. A few moments later, I was informed of everything that had taken place in the town during my absence. The most worrisome piece of news was that the gendarme Reines had greeted Mother in the street with the piercing look of a Gestapo officer, instead of with his previous polite hello. That seemed to underline the possibility that he knew or guessed who we were. Of course, I tried to diminish the importance of this in front of Mother, I thought. Mother immediately told me about how persecuted she felt by Reines's hateful glance and that various little things the mayor had been saying led her to conclude that he gave credence to the rumors spread by Reines.

Life went on as before. Every passing minute separated us farther and farther from that fateful date of February 7, 1941, when Mother had learned from the mayor's secretary that Reines had told the mayor about the Jewish woman, working in Rayon Verwaltung. The hope that the enemy might have forgotten about us grew in proportion to the time that went by.

Soon, a new danger was hanging over our heads. A new regulation was announced concerning the so-called "passportization," that is, the issuing of new identity documents to all. This was connected to the verification of existing documents, birth certificates, and so forth. Our birth certificates were so poorly falsified that we were afraid to show them. In addition, I didn't have even a temporary identity card, as only Mother had received one during her stay in Sworotwa. I was supposed to leave for Swojatycze again. The perpetual fear was backed by the very real threat that, after all, it was very easy to prove who I was!

The last evening with my family arrived. It was hard to part with them, knowing that was for a long time or perhaps forever. As we chatted about various things, trying to prolong the evening, we suddenly heard loud explosions in the distance, and the entire house trembled. They're bombing, they're bombing! We were overcome with joy. What a holiday! Not far from us, justice was being dealt to the persecutors. Oh, if only there were a few more explosions. We could hear the buzz of plane engines. Those were free people up there! Oh, to be with them! A blissful feeling spread in my heart.

My thoughts traveled up, toward our saviors, toward the people who need not fear the Gestapo because of the terrible tradition of circumcision. What a drastic difference between their possible deaths and ours! *After all, it's nothing to die for freedom,"* I thought, and I could picture myself for a moment free, happy, sitting in an airplane. I smiled to myself. I listened eagerly to every buzzing of an engine. It was to me what the Mass is to a Christian. I prayed to the buzzing engines: "Oh, you, the Free Ones, free us from our slavery." We would kiss them to pieces, these pilots, these brothers of humanity who fought with the devil Hitler.

And once more, just like a week earlier, the many dozens of kilometers of road to Swojatycze were ahead of me. I got a ride with the same estate manager with whom I had ridden the week before. When we arrived at his estate, it was completely dark. I accepted his cordial invitation to dinner and to stay overnight.

In the morning, the manager's son gave me a lift in his sleigh all the way to Swojatycze. It was sunny and even a little warm. The snow on the roofs was melting. My mood was not bad because the weather was beautiful. Wyszek greeted me very cordially, without expressing any surprise over the appearance of an unexpected guest for the second time. The room was sunny and warm. The sun poured in with broad rays.

"Why, it's spring!" Wyszek exclaimed and opened the window. Water trickled down from the roof in thin rivulets, and the sparrows were singing with a vengeance. All this signaled the end of winter. And I, after all, had been dreaming of the coming of spring. In the spring it's always possible to escape, to hide somewhere, as long as frost and snow are gone—the worst enemies of those chased and of the poor. And here I was alive, and spring was coming.

The seventh of February, that terrible day of the news about the denunciation, seemed at this point to be very distant, even though in reality only a little over a month had gone by since then. But ahead of me there was a new danger: passportization. My mother and my sister, even if suspected, could not be unequivocally proven "guilty" on the spot, but I would be the cause of their and my own demise—only Jewish males were circumcised. The school ID, my only document, was insufficient to obtain a passport. So what could I count on? I knew I had to leave at all costs. Perhaps in a large city like Warsaw, it would be easier to hide. In addition, I was counting on the greater tolerance of people in Poland.

We were supposed to leave for Baranowicze a few days later. Quite unexpectedly, the Platers arrived from Sworotwa. They, too, were on their way to Baranowicze. We went there all together on a cloudy, snowy day. I felt quite confident in such "Aryan" company. I walked all over town with Wyszek in an attempt to obtain the pass, but there had been no change in their issuance since the previous week. My only possibility was to get to Warsaw illegally, which looked very uncertain and did not attract me in the least. And so we returned empty-handed to Swojatycze. Again, just as after the first failure to leave, I felt relieved that I did not go and did not abandon my family. On the way back,

Jan entertained me with hunting stories from before the war. I was completely calm, but the calm went away when I remembered the ongoing passportization.

Wyszek assured me that since my mother worked in the office of the magistrate, she would be able to procure such a document for me without any trouble. The arrival of a friend of Wyszek, a member of the Armia Krajowa (Home Army—the Polish Underground), changed things once again. It was decided that I would leave with him for Warsaw. There, I would be left to my own devices. I was ready to go, even though in the depths of my soul, I was completely against it. I wished to see my family again and to check at the same time on the progress of passportization. Time pressed. Wyszek's friend was to leave the following day. There was no means of transportation by which I could make it back to Horodyszcze. Wyszek suggested I go by bicycle. I thought with horror about trying to cover dozens of kilometers of snowed-over roads on a bike. Already the first turns of the pedals convinced me of the fantastic nature of such an undertaking, but I tried anyhow, and I spent more time on the ground than on the bicycle. The road was impassable. The following day, I was on my way to Horodyszcze, but in a sleigh—and with the thought of staying there.

Another teary welcome and the warmth of home surrounded me. Mother showed me the passport she had received. I thought to myself that I would be the happiest man on earth if I could be in the possession of such a document. We decided that the following day, in the absence of the mayor, we would take care of the passport for me. Oh, if only that would go well, then the great danger would recede, or, perhaps, it would be gone completely. We would then be able to spend the rest of the war quietly in Horodyszcze. We slept fitfully.

The following morning, Mother took my school ID with her. It was in the shape of a little book with a hard cover. We removed the cover, and the two white pages—the first and the last—gave from a distance the impression of a folded birth certificate, necessary to obtain a new ID. The mayor's secretary was replacing him that day. When Mother placed my folded ID in front of him, he pushed it away and said, "Nye treba," ("It's not necessary") to show Mother that he trusted her. With what joy Mother brought me the completed passport-ID application and told me about how she got it. Now it only had to be stamped in a local office, but that was easy because the "wojt" did not require birth certificates from the people he knew. Still, I was a bit nervous. But the stamping went very smoothly, and I became the proud owner of a real passport-ID issued by the authorities, in which, under the rubric "nationality," was written *Pole*.

Photo from the Vilnius (Wilno) high school identification before the German Occupation. In the summer of 1941 during the Occupation, this document continued to be my ID, after we changed my name on it from Dynin to Dunin and the year of my birth from 1925 to 1929.

*Photo of Franciska "Dunin" that was attached to the ID document
during the German Occupation of Gorodysce (Horodyszcze).
The so-called "Paszportyzacja" started in
Gorodysce in the early spring of 1942.*

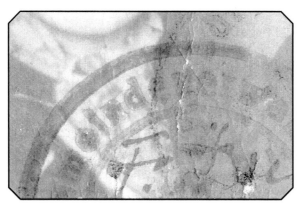

*The entire population was required to apply for new ID documents.
They needed to bring their birth certificates and photos. The photo
of my mother was stamped with two stamps: a blue one from
the office of the mayor ("Bürgermeister") and a red one from the
county office ("Gemeindeverwaltung"). Both stamps are legible.
Mother's partial signature ("F. Du" from F. Dunin) is visible.*

CHAPTER SEVEN

IT WAS THE SPRING of 1942. Slowly everything was becoming green. Sticky buds of the chestnut tree were cracking and showing their contents. We were feeling more light-hearted, but our peace of mind evaporated any time the gendarme Reines appeared in town. At such times, Mother tried to stay out of his way and took a roundabout route to the office, walking through the gardens.

In the backyard of our house, there was a destroyed vegetable and fruit garden, and even though we did not allow ourselves to think that the war might last longer than that year, we, nonetheless, decided to take advantage of this wonderful opportunity to grow our own vegetables. Every day, I dug up the soil until the space resembled a garden again. I was still only a beginning gardener, and I left an empty area where I intended to put in some potatoes. The neighbor with whom we had shared the house had left, and we were now completely alone. We decided to move to the other room, which, even though it was small (it was no wider than 2.5 meters), was more cozy and seemed cleaner than ours. The entrance was through the yard, which was to our liking as our goal was to be seen as little as possible.

One day, over a dozen Poles were arrested in the rich village of Przewloki, near Horodyszcze. This was the first time that the Poles from the area felt some degree of the power of their German "liberators."

When, several days later, the arrested men had not returned from the interrogations, their families asked my mother to write "requests." In return, they brought us hens, eggs, and cheese—all much needed after our feeble winter fare. A week later, all the arrested men were released, and their families were always grateful to us for the favorable response to their requests.

Rumors began to circulate in town that all those without employment would be taken to Germany for forced labor. Mother signed me up to work in the forest. This was an excellent choice. Because the work hours were all day long, I was out of town and hence out of enemy sight. Early in the morning, I would leave for the forest with a whole band of boys, with axes on our backs. The forest was four kilometers away, and we had to go through two villages to get there. The area was lovely—hills covered with woods. Twice a day, we passed through the picturesque village of Jasieniec, situated by a lake and surrounded by woods. I don't remember the name of the second village. The forest was mixed and very dense, full of birds and wild animals. It seemed to offer an inexhaustible supply of timber. Our group soon began its destructive work. Daily, we cut down several pine trees, trimmed their branches off, and cut the logs for timber; we also arranged the remnant wood into stacks. This was the first serious physical labor of my life, and I got tired very quickly, while the balsamic air of the forest induced me to sleep. I came home tanned, in a great mood, and with an even greater appetite. I wore no hat on purpose so that my hair would be bleached by the sun. I looked 100 percent Aryan.

Soon, the logging stopped, and our group was dismantled. I found work in the forest district office as an assistant to the secretary. Among the boys with whom I worked in the forest, there was one, Kazik, with whom I became good friends. We discussed literature and society. Once, when the topic was appropriate, I mentioned to him my "aristocratic" origin, and I asked for his discretion. I knew that this was a certain way to have the news spread quickly, especially since our new last name, Dunin, was noble, and everyone knew that we were friends with Count Plater and his relative, the Baroness from the Czernichowiec estate.

Within a week, Kazik managed to inform all in the forest district office about this, and from there, the news reached others in town. This caused us some trouble, as we did not know what to answer when people asked us whether we came from the Borkowskis or from the Wasowicz branch of the Dunin family. We chose the former, just as we had once before, in Woroncza.

The arrival of the gendarme Reines once more destroyed our peace of mind. He was a frequent guest at Dr. Piaskowski's, where he was wined and dined, just as the other local "dignitaries" were, including the police chief, who, it was commonly known, had been a thief before the war. Mrs. Piaskowska mentioned to my mother in passing that Reines had come again to clear the town of Jews.

I can still visualize Reines, standing on the verandah of the mayor's apartment after a copious meal. A short figure with a large stomach and a shiny helmet, he carried a short automatic weapon in his hand. On the same day, fifteen young Jewish men and women were brought in from the Burdakowszczyzna estate. They had worked there for a month, having been brought in from Molczadz. I became sick to my stomach at the very sight of Reines, and I dragged myself home on feeble legs. Mother came from the office also half dead. The fifteen were going to be executed. We heard an automatic gun discharge. Mother's face went pale.

"They're killing innocent people over there," I said to God more than to myself or to Mother. A few minutes later, we heard another discharge. Then a few single shots. It was horrible. We realized that these shots had served to kill off the miserable young lives.

We had no news except for the Nazi paper entitled *Minsker Zeitung*. This was our only source for news from the front, but, of course, we did not trust it. Still we kept reading this paper because there was nothing else to read, and "between the lines" we drew various conclusions, constructing our own version of the true situation on the front. The Germans sent entire propaganda crews, who, via microphones, announced the fantastic successes in Russia and who called on all "Aryans" to cooperate. Influenced by this propaganda, many of the town's inhabitants began to believe in the stability of Hitler's rule.

The Platers' visits were always a pleasant event. We tried to receive them in a most cordial manner, and we treated them to everything we had at home. They would come with Stefan, who invariably cheered us up, as he claimed that the invasion of Europe would begin soon and that in a short time we would be free. From various mathematical-historical brain teasers, it was evident that the year 1942 would be the year of the Germans' failure, and after that the war would last another two years.

The essential thing is that they leave these lands as soon as possible, I thought, *because, after all, one order from Reines to have me examined medically, and we'll be lost.*

Tadeusz, who came to Sworotwa with Stefan, came to see us as well. He told us that in one of the villages, there were already partisans dressed in army uniforms—Poles and Russians—and that he was waiting for the spring to join them. We, too, were waiting for the spring which would bring us warmth, a possibility of escape, and ... the partisans. But ahead of us was another winter that could bring potentially difficult surprises.

The winter was harsh. The Germans ordered a forced collection of warm clothes for their "heroes" who were freezing on the eastern front. People brought gloves, scarves, and sheepskin coats so that the Germans would leave them in peace and wouldn't suspect them of opposing the regime. Some brought things out of gratitude for the "liberation."

We had enough firewood that year because I brought from the forest as much as I wanted to. We heated the place to our hearts' content, and we delighted in the warmth, while outside there was a snowstorm and the dry, biting frost. People said they could not recall such frost. All the storage areas containing "post-Jewish" clothes were opened, and the things were divided among the police. I saw one of the policemen, known for having been a "hero" of the slaughter in Horodyszcze, throwing comforters on a wagon in front of one of those storage areas. Feathers were flying from the cut pillows, and down filled the air. This made a terrible impression on me.

A month later, this policeman "hero" got sick with typhoid. That began an epidemic. Every day, the sick were brought in from the region. In our town, there were also cases of the disease. The sick and the dying lay in the small "hospital" run by Dr. Piaskowski. The doctor's pantries and his chicken coop filled up nicely as the families of the sick peasants brought him whatever he wanted in exchange for better care. For us, the time of the typhoid fever was a very threatening period. If I had gotten sick, we would have been lost because I would fall into the hands of the doctor. I could imagine such a scenario, and we even wondered whether it would be possible to bribe him with the few remaining jewels we had, but we decided that he would denounce us later anyhow.

This was our psychosis during the entire period of the Nazi occupation: the continual fear and thoughts about the future. We perceived every petty detail as directed against us. Hence, we made every effort to keep away from the "venomous" lice, the carrier of the disease. We avoided other people's apartments; I even endeavored not to touch anyone. Several months passed under the menace of the epidemic.

I remember when the Germans built a gallows on the square in front of the church. It was visible through a small window in the front of our house. I could see the people from nearby villages who were hanged there. According to the Germans, they had collaborated with the partisans. They were left hanging there for all the inhabitants of Horodyszcze to see. It was a horrible sight beyond description—we were simply afraid to look through the window.

At about the same time, the first news came at last about the partisans themselves. They were still not very numerous and occupied themselves mostly with confiscating food. We hoped to make it to the summer and join them. At the time, I was already working as the gamekeeper's aid and then as the gamekeeper because he was afraid of the partisans and didn't want to work outside of the town. Every day, I walked or rode the gamekeeper's black horse to the forest, which was several kilometers away. Sometimes the snow was up to the my knees. Just as before, I measured the logs of wood with the other gamekeeper, Wasia. The logs were then sold to the peasants by the forest district office. To get a "better" measure of wood, the peasants brought us vodka and snacks. I drank eagerly because of the cold and because I wanted to show that I knew how to drink "like a Pole."

When spring came, the forest was suddenly filled with lots of little flowers. For me, spring brought hope and a brighter turn of mind, but Mother was inconsolable and didn't always believe in the possibility of survival. I was her consolation, and I tried to believe in what I thought. The danger was not over. The Piaskowskis, Reines, or other people who, we believed, suspected us of being Jewish could destroy us. We were at peace only in our sleep, and we were always waiting for this sleep, which allowed us to escape from our reality. The trees had become green, and the forest was beautiful.

On my way to work every day, I passed by a group of girls who walked to school from Jasieniec. Among them one distinguished herself: she was taller than the others, very pretty, and wore braids. By virtue of passing each other every day and smiling at each other, we ended up meeting. Her name was Jaga, and she was the daughter of the Jasieniec village administrator. I had no intention of flirting with her or with any other girl. I held myself to a harsh discipline and fought every erotic thought that sprouted in my mind. This was a hard struggle at my age, but I won it with the strength of my will.

Halfway through the summer, the partisan activity increased significantly. The partisans burned several administration buildings in the small towns near Horodyszcze. A number of executions of the civil servants of the "New Europe" by the partisans in the area caused a mass arrival of such people to Horodyszcze, where they felt safer because of the greater German presence. One day, a partisan came to town and surrendered himself to the police. Mother was called in to translate. The partisan said that he had escaped from his unit because he didn't believe his struggle made any sense. After imprisoning him for a few days, the Germans released him, and he was to serve in the police. The gendarmes said that such people made excellent policemen. Soon after his arrival, the town was attacked for the first time. It was at night. The partisans used a heavy machine gun. We hid in the cellar to escape from the bullets of our "liberators."

Mother and I were of the opinion that the partisan who had appeared of his own volition must be on our side, and the attack on the town was his first success since his "crossing over" to the German side. That meant that he had some means of communicating with the partisans and had supplied them with necessary information.

Horodyszcze soon took on a different aspect. Bunkers were being constructed in the town center, and barbed wire entanglements were put up. The local garrison consisted of seven German gendarmes and thirty local policemen who were known as "Black Ravens" on account of of their black uniforms.

We derived great satisfaction from all the good news concerning the partisan activity. They entered towns, burned offices, and killed those devoted to the new regime (collaborators). They attacked police stations, stealing arms and munitions. Soon the small partisan groups grew into entire "otryady" (units). We heard most of all about "Grozny" and "Pyervomayski." The results followed soon. Horodyszcze began to grow in population and became akin to an island in the sea of partisans.

Wasia Winogradow, the gamekeeper whose job I had in the forest, was quickly scared away from his own village. He arrived with his whole family in Horodyszcze, and his brother became the registrar at the registrar's office, where marriage licenses were issued. In addition to the official fee, the marriage license required a payment in vodka and pork fat to the registrar. The Winogradows took a room in the house where we were living. Originally, our cohabitation was agreeable. The old Mrs. Winogradowa gave us a liter of milk a day and occasionally some eggs. It was not possible to anticipate that this family would play such an important role in the life of the town and of many families.

This was a period of relaxation for us, and we abandoned the project of escaping to join the partisans; it would have been very risky anyhow on account of my little sister. At the same time, food was very scarce.

On my way to the forest, peasants would invite me home for bread and milk because they could tell by my countenance that I was suffering from hunger. The bread they baked tasted like ginger bread, and the cool, sweet milk was like nectar. I realized then what nourishment was to the body. As I ate and drank, my entire body warmed up, and strength returned to my muscles. By that time, I had replaced the gamekeeper in all his duties. I was the one who issued wood to the peasants, and after a while, I learned how to use that fact to my advantage.

As I have already mentioned, I led a very austere kind of life, banishing all erotic thoughts from my mind. For example, one day I was walking or riding to work when near Jasieniec, on a hill, I saw a familiar figure. It was Jaga. She was wearing a light, homespun dress and a colorful kerchief on her head. The wind lifted her dress high, revealing her lovely shape. "Puydee syudi, puydee syudi," ("Come here, come here.") she called out to me and motioned with her hand for me to come. "I have no time," I answered, and I rode on.

I often went to the wood-distiller's works. I became friends with the wood-distiller, a poor man with a very unkempt wife and five children. Misery and dirt emanated from every corner of the wood distillery. The distiller told high tales about the Germans' losses. He claimed that the Russians were no more than a few dozen kilometers away from us. Despite the passage of time, however, this distance remained constant. I went to see this man with various orders from the main forester, who, out of fear of the partisans, did not venture into the forest. My daily work in the open air gave me a ruddy complexion and made my hair flaxen. I had the appearance of a typical Pole, and my slightly longish nose was attributed to aristocratic rather than any other reasons. As a matter of fact, I dropped hints that the septum had been broken when I used to practice boxing.

Around that time, the family of the organ player Kolwicz came to Horodyszcze. I met his exceptionally beautiful daughter. Dark-haired, with white, well-groomed hands, lovely cheeks, large eyes, small lips, and a pretty figure, she made a great impression on me. Previously, I had seen such marvels only in pictures. Human nature, on the one hand, and my firm resolve to act modestly on the other: the two struggled with each other. The struggle was all the harder because the girl was beautiful and provocative. Sometimes we went to the woods together to pick lilies of the valley. The forest was simply white with the flowers, and their fragrance intoxicated us. This idyll would have been undisturbed if not for merciless mosquitoes. I was bleeding in several places.

"Look, your blue blood is no different from ordinary blood," she said half jokingly. I took it as testimony to my success—the news of my being a count, which I had confided a while back to Kazik in greatest secret, had spread far. In the forest, she tried to convince me to sit down next to her, and she cuddled up to me with great fervor. Often she invited me to her house when no one was there. She played the mandolin sweetly and then kissed me, whispering that she was in love with me. At last, after she failed to make me into her lover, she stopped seeing me. She paid me back in the following manner: afterward she was always seen in the company of Major Zigling, the chief of the police battalion who was known as the "De Luxe" bandit, and about whom I will have occasion to speak later. Having learned about their relationship, I couldn't help imagining her in the arms of this terrible and cruel German. For some time, I thought of nothing else.

One day, all the Jewish translators in the town were arrested. When, a few hours later, police went to the ghetto to get their families, we knew at once what that meant: their fate was sealed. That was the Germans' tactic—the victims' families had to be destroyed as well, so as not to leave enemies. We lived through a period of great anxiety because one of those translators knew that we were Jewish. He was the man in whom the countess had confided in Sworotwa.

"I'm convinced that his wife, too, knows about us," said Mother. "She will want to save herself, and she'll tell the Germans about us."

A man faced with death is ready to do anything to please his sick optimism, if only there is a glimmer of hope, however unreal, I thought. Each moment seemed to bode ill for us. After all, it was quite possible that the translator's wife would break down and tell the executioners about us.

This was a very real possibility that made me throw myself down on my knees before God. I prayed incessantly that we might be spared any ill fortune, and, for the time being, we were spared.

I was on very good terms with the priest. The priest and his housekeeper were intelligent people who received me very kindly. I discussed many social topics with the priest, who had rather progressive views that were shared by the housekeeper. No wonder that the rectory's atmosphere was soothing to me. In town, we tried to give the impression of being very poor because no one envies the poor, and therefore they have few enemies. This was made easier by the fact that we, indeed, barely managed to make ends meet. What we lacked most was clothing. I had one shirt, which Mother washed on Saturday so that I would have it clean for Sunday. As for food, we were now well supplied—we had vegetables from the garden, and Mother earned extra items, such as butter, eggs, and cheese, by translating requests. I brought home various kinds of food from the peasants in exchange for the wood, and we also received food as a gift before the holidays from the priest, for example, an entire basked filled with victuals. He considered us to be a decent Polish family in need. Every year before Easter, he asked me to come with him to all the villages in the area, where he blessed the Easter food baskets. We returned from these trips loaded with kielbasa, fat, eggs, smoked meat, and so forth. I tried to return his kindness by gathering mushrooms for him in the forest and sending firewood to the rectory. I experienced Sundays with my entire being. I went to church dressed in clean clothes, often in a damp shirt and wet (freshly washed) socks.

As time went on, I began to have a fairly good sense of religious practice. I knew that the slightest mistake could betray me. My little sister was friends with the neighbors' daughter and imitated her in everything, including going to confession and taking communion. Mother was the one who fared the worst in church. Often, watching her from a distance, I would see her make mistakes in the prayers: she didn't cross herself on time, and she forgot to kneel at the proper times in the service. I looked at our neighbors anxiously to see if they, too, had noticed. Mrs. Piaskowska, the doctor's wife, was the person who prayed most fervently of all. She stayed on her knees for a long time and beat her breast while reciting litanies.

The church was always clean and smelled of incense. Through a small window in the roof, we could see a tree branch that served as a perfect natural calendar. In winter, the little windowpane was covered with hoarfrost, or I could see snow on the branch. That was when our existence was threatened the most because, in case of danger, we could not hide anywhere or escape. I prayed for God to allow us to see green in that little window. Spring came at last, and the church was adorned with fresh flowers, which rendered the daily services quite pleasant. Golden rays of sunlight filled the church, and the fragrance of flowers mixed with incense, creating a soothing calm. The priest, in an embroidered chasuble, and his two helpers in white added to the whole.

Sunday was to me a day of perfect rest. I didn't look for company, preferring to wander on my own. With a book in hand, I walked in the fields or in the meadows, day-dreaming. I was close to God, and I connected all the events of the day with him. He seemed to be near, and I trusted in Him completely, forgoing all fear. I thought how good it would be if Mother, too, trusted in God; she wouldn't be so depressed and anxious whenever a real or fictitious danger loomed near. I returned home from Mass when the sun was already setting. I always tried to avoid serving at Mass because I was afraid to make a fool of myself. When no one volunteered to serve, the priest would come out in front of the church and "catch" those boys who were late to be his helpers. No one could refuse him. Aware of this, I always came to Mass a few minutes early, thus avoiding such a possibility.

But one afternoon after dinner when I was passing next to the rectory, I was stopped by the priest. "I'm so glad to see you. I need someone badly to serve at a wedding Mass."

I felt ill at ease. I wasn't sure when to ring the little silver bell, when to kneel, when to stand up, and so on. Nonetheless, I could not refuse, so I went into the sacristy with him, and I put on the white robe. Fortunately, the other boy who served at Mass arrived at the last minute. He was young and not very tall, but he was an expert in the service. The church filled with people, attending the ceremony. All the clerks of the Rayon where Mother worked were there.

The marriage was between the vice-mayor Laciszonek and a Polish teacher. I knew the young woman to be intelligent and a great Polish patriot, while Laciszonek was frequently sent by the mayor to execution sites as the "observer representing the mayor." I remember that after coming back from an "action" in Stolowicze, Laciszonek said, "daly mnye vintoovkoo v rookie ee ya tozhe strelal" (they put a gun in my hands and I shot too"). Thus I was one of the three people officiating at the marriage of one of my mortal enemies. The priest came out first, while I, having tripped on the rug in the sacristy, practically landed on the altar. That was the auspicious beginning of the ceremony. I was under the impression that the eyes of all those present focused on me, and I felt faint. The bride and the groom were married with plenty of curses that I did not spare Laciszonek, saying them under my breath. If someone had watched me closely, they would have noticed that my ringing was always somewhat delayed in respect to the ringing of the other altar boy. I imitated everything he did, and, consequently, there was a short lag between his and my motions.

These were the last days of the summer. We no longer had any illusions as to a quick end of the war. The German newspapers were filled with accounts of successes of the German army, even though they mentioned no new territorial gains. That led us to believe that the lines of the front were stable. One day, a wave of anti-Semitic articles began to flood the papers. We knew what that meant: before every large-scale execution, the Germans tried to mold the public opinion against the Jews. The Jews remaining in the Horodyszcze ghetto worked as artisans or helped in the demolition of old houses. Once, seeing Jews who were dismantling a house, I walked up to them and addressed one in Polish so that no one would notice: "What are you counting on? They won't leave you alone."

I received the following answer: "I've been put against the wall to be shot already three times, and I was saved. So if I am to live, I will live."

A few days later, and only a day or two before the "action," I had the opportunity to communicate with some other inhabitants of the ghetto. I saw two men standing next to the well, which was near our house. I had to act quickly. I ran out into the street and walked up to the well. Slowly, I began to turn the handle as if I were getting water. I lowered my head, so it wouldn't be visible because it was in the well, and I said to them, "Run away! They can come to get you any minute Why don't you escape to the forest?"

The answer I got was similar to the first one: "What is in store for me, shall be. God will save me."

The other man added: "Among our people, one scares the other by saying that in the forest there will be nothing to eat, and we'll starve to death there."

From what happened later, I guessed that perhaps they accepted the idea of escape after all. One day, I would be happy to meet someone who survived the Horodyszcze ghetto. Did a single Horodyszcze Jew survive?

I remember the day Mother came from the office and told me a terrible story. One of the village administrators who always came to the mayor with various denunciations brought the news of a Jewish hideout. The mayor, eager for strong emotions, went there with the police. Seven men and one woman were hiding in a covered up dugout. "The woman screamed that she was Polish!" the mayor said, laughing upon his return. Mother learned later that the mayor, Aleksander Jakimowicz, shot her himself.

In 1945, after our arrival in Lodz, I went to the city hall to find him and hand him over to justice. His permanent address was in Lodz; that was where he had lived with his wife before leaving for Belarus. From the information I was given, it appeared that he had left for Germany just before the end of the war, and I never heard of him again.

Just as we had foreseen, soon there were "actions" consisting of murdering the remaining Jews. The town of Molczadz fell first. The fat gendarme "Gustaw," accompanied by the Belorussian police, was the one who killed miserable, helpless people there. Then the wave of annihilation passed through Horodyszcze. It took place after dinner. All of a sudden, police arrived from the entire area. I was working in the garden when I heard single shots. The police were nearby, at the Kreislandwirt's, where there were Jewish women workers. "This is the end of your life!" I heard the policeman scream to one of the victims in Belorussian. In the streets, we could hear people running away, and others chasing them, as well as shots. A few minutes after the shots had died down, we saw policemen loaded with things they had pillaged in the ghetto. On the main square in front of the church, there were seven corpses. For the first time, the townspeople had a chance to see the results of the slaughter.

Even those who had taken most of the things left by the victims of the first executions were impressed and gloomy. Mr. Kupjanczyk, the owner of a restaurant on the church square and of a sizeable amount of formerly Jewish property, walked back and forth nervously and said, "This cannot go over so smoothly." Soon a car arrived from Baranowicze with "experts" who came to see whether the execution had been conducted "properly." As it turned out, they were very displeased that some Jews had been killed on the square "without a plan," instead of having been gathered and killed all together in one spot. The policemen explained that the Jews were running away. I also learned later that the policemen complained that the Jews had somehow found out about the "action" beforehand, and some of them had escaped before it began.

Following this execution, the chief of police was arrested, and later reports spoke of his having been executed himself. The Germans did not tolerate any single police chief for very long because those were the people who knew the most about the atrocities committed against the Jews in Horodyszcze and in the area. As such, they were dangerous witnesses. During our time in Horodyszcze, the police chief was dismissed three times. Nonetheless, everyone was still eager to try their luck. The police chief's wife was the "first lady" of the town:

Dr. Piaskowski bowed down low to her and kissed her hand, while the mayor invited her and her husband to parties.

The last execution cleared Horodyszcze of all Jews. The ghetto did not exist. Several of the Jews who had escaped before the "action" came back after a few days and asked … to be killed.

As a response to intense partisan activity in the area, the Germans sent the "Ukrainian Battalion" to Horodyszcze. Ten percent of it consisted of Volksdeutsches, while the rest were Russians, Belorussians, Ukrainians, Cossacks, and several Poles. After its arrival, the Battalion was called the Police Battalion. They had several armored vehicles, while other soldiers went by horse or wagon. The Battalion was headed by Major Zigling, a tall, handsome Kraut known for his cruelty. The results of the Battalion's arrival were soon obvious. Villages suspected of cooperation with the partisans were surrounded and burned, while all the inhabitants were murdered. People said that during one such action, Major Zigling raped a young girl and then had her thrown into a burning house. Small children were treated just like the Jewish children. Soldiers took them by the legs and cracked their heads. Soon part of the police force and the Battalion went to the area of the Nalibocka Virgin Forest, where most of the population was Polish-Catholic. Many rich villages were turned into conflagration sites and cemeteries. Many villagers saved themselves by escaping to the partisans.

Not far from Horodyszcze, in the village of Koldyczewo, the Germans built a prison. Its garrison consisted of special S.D. ("Sicherdienst" or security services) police, dressed in gray uniforms. Soon Koldyczewo made its name. In addition to the prison, there also was a large Jewish camp there, which was being liquidated bit by bit every day. In winter, the victims were asked to take off all their clothes and then lie down on the sleighs one on top of another. They were ultimately thrown into a large pit and then killed. All the information we had about Koldyczewo came from the peasants who worked there as "szarawark" (an unpaid forced labor). It was well-known that, among the Jews in Koldyczewo, there was a famous professor of medicine. People came from all over Belarus to be treated by him, having first paid a fee to the S.D. Then one day we learned that all the Jews from Koldyczewo had escaped. We imagined the Germans' fury when they realized that their victims had gotten away. We were certain that the partisans must have helped in this case. This was the only good piece of news in those days.

Someone informed the mayor that the doctor in Stolowicze was Jewish. The mayor called him into the "Rayonova Uprava," and the poor man never returned to his wife in Stolowicze. His wife was Polish, and he claimed to be Polish as well. He was, as far as I can remember, short and a bit stooped. The mayor quickly called an ad hoc committee consisting of three doctors, who determined that the offender was circumcised. He explained to them that in his youth he had suffered from a venereal disease and had had to undergo an operation on the penis. His death was sealed. He was murdered by the police chief Glaszczyk, a former cobbler in the town. Mother heard that Glaszczyk later told others about the deed: "zatrepotal kak pticka i pol" ("he fluttered like a bird and fell").

Tymczasowy Zarząd Miejski w Łodzi
Wydział Ewidencji Ludności

Karta informacyjna

1) Nazwisko *Jakimowicz mgr Aleksander*
2) Imię *Eugeniusz m. Horadziuk*
3) Imiona rodziców
4) Wiek *15. 6. 91 r.*
5) Zawód
6) Poprzedni adres *Piotrkowska 182*

W razie braku imienia osoby poszukiwanej — informacyi
nie udziela się; w razie braku dalszych personalii —
informacyi udziela się tylko w miarę możności.

Na podstawie danych meldunkowych, znajdujących się w kartotece adresowej *zameld. dn. 20.7.44 przy ul. Piotrkowskiej 182 i dn. 9. 10. 44 wymeld. do Mahla - Turyngie*

9. 19 *45* r.

ale zamieszkałych w Łodzi
ści nie jest notowana.
wywane są w kartotece

[podpis]
c urzędnika udzielającego informacyi.

Back in Lodz after liberation, I started to look immediately for Aleksander Jakimowicz, who was a war criminal in our eyes. Jakimowicz was from Lodz. According to information from City Hall in Lodz, he arrived in Lodz on July 20, 1944, from Horodyszcze and left for Mahla-Turyngia in Germany on October 9, 1944.

Neuchâtel, le 27th. December, 1943.

Dear Sir,

    We received your lines of the 10th. of October and have since written to Mrs. Dynin.

    The letter was addressed as before, but has been returned to us as Mrs. Dynin is evidently no longer staying at the previous address.

    Under the circumstances you will understand that we cannot do anything further for you.

    We remain, dear Sir,

                Yours faithfully,

              EDOUARD DUBIED & Cᴵᴱ
                  SOCIÉTÉ ANONYME

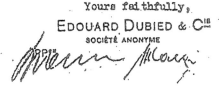

EDOUARD DUBIED & Cᴵᴱ
SOCIÉTÉ ANONYME
NEUCHATEL (SUISSE)
COMPTE DE CHÉQUES
ET VIREMENTS IV 252
TÉLÉPHONE Nᵒ 5.23.22 et 5.23.23
111/362
Service VI/OM

Mr. Jacob Bernstein
P. O. Box 2071.

T e l - A v i v

Palestine.

*The front and back of a letter-card, dated 27 December 1943.
Note the stamps of the Swiss Post Office, along with the German
and British (Palestine) censorship. As my father was representing
the firm of Edouard Dubied & Cie in Poland and was a good
friend of Mr. Dubied, Mr. Bernstein, whose family we had known
for many years, inquired with Dubied about us. Note that, at that
time, we had already been in Gorodysce for almost two years.*

CHAPTER EIGHT

THE YEAR WAS 1944. The winter was not as harsh as the previous one. We had enough firewood. The best oak and birch wood was stocked in our yard. We also had plenty of food because I sold the wood designated for the Germans to the peasants in exchange for meat and pork fat. The forester knew about the dealings, but he didn't do anything about it because he himself got quite rich by selling construction timber to the peasants without German permission. Once, the German gendarmerie in town requested firewood from the forest district office. They wanted a lot of wood for themselves and for the police, so instead of picking it up at the forestry ground, they went themselves, heavily escorted, to the forest. Of course, as the forester, I was supposed to go with them to show them the way to the wood, and, naturally, I wasn't looking forward to that. I knew that not much wood was left there because in the last months I had exchanged most of it for moonshine and pork fat.

There were about thirty wagons in our party. The gendarmes and the policemen were armed to the teeth and had their machine guns ready in case we ran into the partisans. They seated me on the first wagon so that I could show them where to go. Since we were quite a military force, I was hoping that the partisans would not attack on the way into the forest, but rather would get ready and attack us on the way back. Of course, when we arrived at the place where the firewood was supposed to be stacked in "meters," there was hardly anything there, even less than I had thought, because people had stolen it without my knowledge. Out of the thirty wagons, we were able to load only four.

The Germans were furious and asked, "Where is the promised wood?"

My answer was ready: "It was stolen by the partisans."

On the way back, they saw a human figure crossing a field toward the forest. The Germans decided to have a bit of a shoot-out in that direction. I knew that the person, whoever it was, managed to hide in the forest, and the Germans stopped shooting.

The new Kreislandwirt Budyna, who was a citizen of Ireland, permitted the town clerks to buy piglets at the official rate of several Deutsch marks. We bought a piglet, but as we didn't have any feed for it, we gave it to the neighbors on the condition that they would give us half when they slaughtered it. This gave us a prospect of meat and fat as well as the external impression that we were like everyone else, because all Poles in town raised pigs.

By order of the regional doctor and with the support of the mayor, a public bathhouse was being constructed in Horodyszcze. When it was ready, every inhabitant of the town was supposed to attend it. Once again, danger was looming close, and all peace of mind left us. Dr. Piaskowski also claimed that he had to examine everyone in town because of the ostensible possibility of venereal disease. Once more, the tradition of circumcision brought us close to death. The bathhouse was almost finished, and the threat was imminent. We had survived so much, and now we were supposed to give up?

It was the midst of winter, and everything was covered in deep snow. The situation appeared hopeless. We considered the following possibilities:

1. We would go to the bathhouse and submit to the medical examination.

2. I would escape.

3. All three of us would escape.

The first possibility signified certain death. Dr. Piaskowski, who, we thought, suspected us of being Jewish anyhow, would pay special attention to my member and would report us to Reines. Also, in the bathhouse, anyone could notice that I was "different" because one had to be naked in there. On the other hand, if I disappeared from Horodyszcze on my own, the Germans would consider it an "escape to join the bandits" (i.e., the partisans), and even if I managed to get to the partisans, the Germans would kill my mother and sister. I couldn't risk that. Only the third prospect gave us a chance, assuming we could put it into practice.

But how? The partisan area began with the village of Koniaszczowczyzna, which could be reached through the forest where I worked. But even though I knew a lot of peasants in the villages through which we'd have to pass, it seemed wiser to take a different route because it would look suspicious if all of a sudden Mother, my little sister, and I started walking toward the forest—and the Germans would know about it in a matter of hours. The roundabout way led through the road to Nowogrodek, and then one had to turn to the forest. The difficulty was that we would have to cross half of Horodyszcze. The escape would have to be carried out before nightfall, after Mother arrived from the office. That way, if everything went smoothly, they would not start looking for us until the next morning—when Mother wouldn't show up at work.

The other difficulty was that in the evening, one of the Winogradows could stop by to borrow something or to ask about something. This was a fairly common occurrence, despite the fact that our relations with old Mrs. Winogradowa were strained, as she had turned out to be a real witch. The congenial atmosphere she cultivated at first was only a scheme to soften us up. I had a very unpleasant experience with her one day—she came to our room, wanting to take by force our shutters, which she claimed I had stolen from them. When I didn't let her take them, she screamed at me, "Jud!" I didn't know if she meant it literally or if she used it as a slur. In any case, I had to pretend I was insulted, and Mother expressed her "outrage" in a conversation with Misha, her younger son. For several days, I was frightened and worried about this incident. *Is the old hag on to our secret?* I wondered.

All in all, the prospect of escape was not very appealing. To go into the unknown with Mother, who was a weak woman, and with my ten-year-old sister, to walk through the snowed-over fields and woods! What we feared most was getting to these fields and woods. It was nearly impossible to leave the town unnoticed. We also had other thoughts: here it's warm, and there is enough food; why leave all this? We could already picture Mrs. Winogradowa taking our things from our room. Even though none of them were very precious, they were, nonetheless, dear to us because they had accompanied us through so much. We decided not to allow this to happen. We decided to burn our things before running away. We began to burn the less precious things, leaving the better ones to be burned just before the escape. But it was so hard to part with them! I decided to hide some of our belongings in the forest and went looking for a good hiding place for them and for the shortest, most secure roads. I found a large hollow in a tree trunk, perfect for hiding things, and I marked the shortest route with chalk on the tree trunks.

In the meantime, the bathhouse was officially opened, so we had to hurry with our plan. We chose the day. Our souls were heavy. I tried to console Mother as much as I could and to encourage her with my determination. We kept comparing our current situation to what would be happening to us in another day in the forest.

"If this were spring, the whole thing would not be a problem," said Mother, "but now we'll surely perish." We postponed the escape by one day, then by another. On the third day, unexpectedly, the bathhouse burned down. Zigling's Battalion decided to rebuild it, but for themselves, not for civilian use. It was as if God's hand had been in this. Dr. Piaskowski still insisted on the general medical examination, though. We believed that might be on my account and that he wanted to unmask us. Mother made a courageous move. She approached the mayor and told him, "In no country has there been a practice to examine all the inhabitants of an entire town in order to determine whether they were healthy or sick with intimate (venereal) diseases." She suggested that such an action would cause the mayor to be ridiculed. The mayor took this seriously, and there was no more talk of any such examination. Naturally, we felt a little better, but were still depressed by our recent experiences.

Working in the forestry office, I became better friends with Kazik. He was the son of a rich peasant, and he had a high school diploma, which was a rare thing in such a small town. He was an exceptionally intelligent boy with whom I could discuss various matters. Our conversations made him trust me. He was a member of the Armia Krajowa (Home Army or AK), the Polish underground military organization. Thanks to him I, too, had become an official member of the Polish underground already in 1943. Kazik made me swear that I would be in contact only with him and that I would not breathe a word to anyone else in the forest district, even though they were all essentially involved with the underground. My mother was to be the only exception, as he expected me to convey information from her concerning the Germans' visits to Rayon Verwaltung. At least once a week, a German officer would come to see the mayor. Usually it was the Kreislandwirt with his personal translator. They did not interest us. Whenever somebody from the Gestapo came, the mayor closed the door to his office and did not let Mother in, unlike when the visitors were Germans who came to discuss economic matters, even if they had their own translator. Hence, Mother knew of various orders, such as possible round-ups for forced labor in Germany, a day in advance. In this way, we knew at the forest district office that for a day or two, we would have to hide in the wood distiller's shed deep in the forest.

One day, following the visit of the Gestapo men, the mayor was very excited and, perhaps for that reason, left on his desk a piece of paper with two names or pseudonyms on it. Mother found the piece of paper and memorized the names. I ran to tell Kazik about it and found out that they were expecting two important AK officers in Horodyszcze, apparently the Gestapo wanted to catch them. Thanks to the fact that the mayor left that piece of paper on his desk, they were saved because the visit was cancelled at once, although I'm not sure how.

Kazik passed on to me the "Informational Bulletin" and the "Dawn," published by the AK. I read them from cover to cover because such underground papers were considered something sacred. Soon, I was familiar with the AK policy for the eastern borderlands: to help the Germans fight the Soviet partisans and thereby fight Soviet Russia. I learned that the Germans had practically lost the war already, so the remaining enemy was "the Soviets, lying in wait for Poland's independence." When I asked Kazik whether he thought that after the Germans' withdrawal, "we" would be able to resist the Soviets, he answered that we had no other option.

In practice, this policy was realized in Horodyszcze and in the area, if not in the entire Belarus, in the following manner: the forester Tryfonov, who was a former officer in the Polish army and was now a commanding officer in the Home Army for the Horodyszcze region, received arms officially from the Germans for so-called "self-defense." It suited the Germans' purpose that people were willing to risk their lives for the "New Europe" by fighting the "Bolsheviks." The forester did not limit himself to defensive action, though. He organized a spy network among Poles living in the region, and based on information he got from them, he undertook raids against the Soviet partisans. His first success was the killing of two partisans near the village of Przewluka. Soon thereafter, the Germans gave the forester machine guns and more munitions. The forester and his people penetrated deeper and deeper into the area dominated by the partisans, and once, he came back without one of his men. Later I heard them say at the forestry office that "he was killed by a Jew." From that moment on, it was understood that those raids against the partisans were not mere entertainment that everyone joined willingly on horseback, as if going for a hunt, but rather a risky business in which one could lose one's life.

The enthusiasm at the forest district cooled off. I say in the forest district because everyone—except for me (as a count, I was presumably too delicate for this) and Halina, the secretary—participated in the actions. My young age (made even younger in my false papers) and my aristocratic origin did not agree with the hardships of these raids. I was trained in the use of the gun, but they hadn't asked me to carry a gun against the partisans.

At about that time, the Germans mobilized several age groups to create the so-called Belorussian battalion, also designated to fight the partisans. The mobilization included boys a year older than I was, at least "on paper," where I was recorded as younger than my actual age. The newly formed battalion was sent to a village about twenty kilometers from Horodyszcze. The AK was active there as well. One of the units of the new battalion consisted of local AK men equipped with the best horses and armed with the best guns. For some time already, Mother had been telling me about the mayor's anxiety. She was guessing that there were going to be mass arrests. When I repeated this to Kazik, he told me that he was already aware of this from other sources. He went directly to the forester to tell him of the news he had from me, as a confirmation of the information they had received a few hours earlier from Baranowicze.

The forester was visibly nervous and ordered the horses and the arms ready just in case. A day later, Kazik said simply, "We're splitting." He reminded me of my old oath not to share with anyone what I had seen and heard at the forestry office, and he explained to me the forester's plan.

He began like this: "Your task is to remain in town and wait for further orders. You're going to be our man in Horodyszcze." The plan was that all the members of the "self-defense group" were going to go into the forest fully armed, feigning a raid against the partisans. The first company of the Belorussian battalion, which was completely in the hands of the AK, was going to escape with all the machine guns and join the Horodyszcze group headed by Tryfonov. This would create quite a sizeable military force, and, according to Tryfonov's suppositions, the Germans would be forced to negotiate. Tryfonov's conditions for cooperation with the Germans were that they supply the unit with munitions and food. In exchange, the unit would fight the partisans.

This plan was going to be put into practice the following day. I had no idea what to do. I was afraid that the Germans might take revenge on me since I worked at the forestry office. It was clear to me that the Germans would not "negotiate" seriously. That meant fighting against the Germans and, consequently, solidarity with the partisans. Despite the orders I got from Kazik, I was more eager to leave with the forester than to remain behind in Horodyszcze in my new role. So I went to Tryfonov and told him about my desire to join them. He explained that my role was also very important, and he added, "Do you know what difficulties and hardships await you? This isn't for you, my count, but I do not wish to stand in your way. Decide and let Kazik know."

Since the forestry office was out of the way, the preparations for the escape proceeded undisturbed. The forester on horseback accompanied two boys on a cart filled with munitions. They were going to hide the boxes and return. Others, including me, were loading a gun repair workshop onto a large wagon. I found a moment to run to say good-bye to the priest and to his housekeeper. I told them briefly what was going on. "What is Tryfonov thinking? After all, this isn't an uprising yet," said the priest. "Mr. Jurek, you shouldn't go," he added when I was leaving.

And I didn't go. I couldn't leave my mother without her caretaker and her consolation. And again, this saved us. I returned the cartridge pouch that I was carrying since I was supposed to be one of the operating personnel of a machine gun. While at the forestry office, I ran into Kazik and told him about my final decision. In the meantime, the forester was instructing Halina, the secretary, in what to say to the Germans if they asked about what was going on in the forest district. I said my good-byes and wished them luck; they wished me the same, and I went home. I could see that the whole town was in a state of nervous tension. The "self-defense" members stood in groups and discussed things in low voices. Among them, I saw Misha Winogradow, our Belorussian neighbor, who walked from one group to another. *Is he, too, a member of the AK?* I wondered. This seemed improbable. *Too many people know about this plan for it to be successful,* I thought.

Soon after my return from the forestry office, I noticed Wasia Winogradow, the gamekeeper whom I had replaced and who, with his brother Misha and their mother, lived in the same house as we did. I knew that Wasia, a former cavalryman in the Polish army, was also part of the battalion company that was preparing to flee. The fact that Wasia was not with the battalion right now, while Misha was out and about in the streets, made me intuitively understand what was up: treason!

They were both home now, whispering. I put my ear to the door and tried to eavesdrop on their conversation. Mother stood next to me, eager to hear what I relayed to her. From what I could tell, Wasia was the traitor. He was telling his brother that the company of the Belorussian battalion that consisted of AK men had been completely liquidated at the moment when they were ready to flee, sitting fully armed on the wagons. What was still a mystery to me was why the Germans didn't follow suit in Horodyszcze. It would appear that Wasia had informed them only of the action prepared by the Belorussian battalion. Perhaps he didn't know anything else?

The town emptied out; no one was in the streets. Bobko, commandant Zigling's translator, came to the Winogradows and left with Misha. Misha didn't return for several hours, and old Mrs. Winogradowa was crying. When Misha came back, he was wearing a revolver attached to his the belt: his brother Wasia's "merits" had rehabilitated him completely in the eyes of the Germans. Later on, it turned out that he had agreed at once to go over to the Germans' side, and soon the Germans were sending him to arrest his friends of yesterday, which he did scrupulously. That same evening Halina, the forest district office secretary, was arrested. The following day, mass arrests began; if any of the "culprits" escaped, the Germans took revenge on their families. They imprisoned all the wives and parents of the men who escaped. A day later, all the siblings and other relatives were arrested as well. The scale of the arrests was without precedent: as a result, one third of the Poles in Horodyszcze were under lock and key, while the rest were in a panic, including us. We were now suffering both as Poles and as Jews. Arrest for us equaled death because every prisoner had to undergo a medical examination.

For the time being, the prisoners were kept in Zigling's battalion's camp, and others were allowed to bring them food. After five days of arrests, we received news that forester Tryfonov was negotiating with the Germans, and in the evening of that day, the Germans authorized Tryfonov to form a "Polish legion" in the village of Przewluka. This "legion" was supposed to fight the partisans, and the Germans were supposed to supply it with arms, ammunition, and provisions. It was suspect that after such a wave of arrests, the Germans seemed to be "retreating." The following day, Polish youth in green pre-war uniforms appeared in town. They belonged to the forester's unit and had come to Horodyszcze to receive provisions, as the agreement with the Germans stipulated. It was truly uncanny: after years, I again saw the Polish uniform. It was a symbol of freedom, and at the moment I banished all thoughts of their cooperating with the Germans. The police battalion issued them generous provisions; I even saw some wine on the cart with food. Polish youth from the entire area were arriving in the village of Przewluka to join the forester. The Polish uniform was a powerful magnet for these young people, some of whom even ran away from home to join. We suspected that the Germans were trying to weaken the vigilance of the Poles in order to surround them later in Przewluka. It was all the more evident when one considered that the Germans didn't even release the forester's wife or the other prisoners.

Mother played a little comedy in front of the mayor and asked him whether he would still allow me to work in the forest district. "Of course," answered the mayor, and so I went as if to work, although in reality, there was nothing to do there now. One day, Tryfonov arrived at the forestry office to see his old, ailing stepfather, so I had a chance to see him. He asked me what people were saying about the whole matter and how they saw the future. I told him what Mother and I thought: "They want to surround our boys." The forester became very thoughtful and left quickly without saying another word.

Great numbers of Cossacks were passing through Horodyszcze.

Men, women, and children, all armed, rode old carts drawn by emaciated horses. This was the "army" against the partisans, the Germans claimed. The atamans (Cossack leaders) wore long capes, while the rest of the people wore rags. They resembled very impoverished partisans and did not look like a military force. It was hard to understand how they were going to fight the partisans. For three days, literally thousands of them passed through Horodyszcze on their way to Nowogrodek. In passing, they stole whatever had value, and people sighed with relief after they and their militant families were gone with their Cossack hats.

Our expectations were fulfilled. One morning, the Germans brought additional forces from Baranowicze; Vlasovtsy, Cossacks, and German infantry all attacked the forester's unit. The forester was apparently ready for the attack; perhaps my conversation with him influenced him as well, because he managed to escape with most of his men. Nonetheless, the Germans caught seventeen youths and brought them, hands tied in back, into town. A new wave of arrests followed. Misha Winogradow, with Zigling's translator Bobko, arrested all the people whom they had seen talking in the streets to the members of the forester's unit who had come to town for provisions. I thought now how lucky it was that I was never seen in the street with Kazik. I knew it could have been dangerous, had someone noticed it, but I didn't know what I would have done if I had seen Kazik, who, fortunately, never came to town. The forester had organized his visit to the forestry office very discreetly; no one other than his stepfather and I saw him in Horodyszcze. In the end, the Germans arrested people whose only fault was that they were Polish. We felt utterly hopeless. We expected to be arrested any minute and had no idea what to do. Once more, we considered the possibility of escaping to the partisans, but now it was even more risky than before. Zigling's battalion was always in action, and one could run into his people everywhere. What was even worse was that the Germans brought in dogs and could easily track us down. I decided to communicate with forester Tryfonov to ask for his help in escaping.

One day, when I was in the timber yard in front of the forest district office, I noticed a man going by whom I recognized. He was a poor gentry man, who came by now and then, and he was possibly himself a member of the AK. I walked up to him boldly and greeted him. My intuition told me that I could trust him. I explained to him the danger we were in (of course I spoke only of the danger of my arrest as a Pole, without mentioning my fear of being examined by a doctor), and I asked him to inform Tryfonov and to request his help. A peasant who brought some wood to the timber yard told me that the forester was now allied with the partisans, who told him, "Kill the Germans as you used to kill us."

When I came home, I saw that in front of the rectory, there were two Germans in black hats that identified them as the personnel of the armored cars of the battalion. Next to them was Bobko the translator. I understood that they were waiting for the priest to come out. Waiting as well were several people whom they had arrested on the way. I was going to be alone in the house: Mother was still at work, and my sister was at the neighbors. I dashed off to the garden and hid there to observe the situation from afar. I saw the priest walk calmly, prayer book in hand, with his taskmasters. The road led next to our house. They were coming closer. *Now they will stop to take me,* I thought. *They want to destroy all the Poles, so they won't spare us either.* I took a deep breath when they went by.

We lived in such a terrible state all day long every day, and each day seemed like an eternity. I tried to avoid going in the street. I went out only to fetch water or to go to work. Once, at work, I noticed Bobko, who, with armed Ukrainians, was approaching the forestry office. And again I thought they were coming to get me. I hid among the stacks of wood. As it turned out, the subject of arrest this time was the single horse left in the forestry office. Bobko laughed out loud, "This time we're arresting a horse!"

In the end, we were one of the very few remaining "Catholic" families in town untouched by the enemy, but for us, too, a trap was set. One day, a peasant came to our little room. I knew he was from one of the nearby villages because he had come several times for wood. His appearance was disgusting: he was short, with small, shrewd eyes and black hair. He brought with him a sense of dread. I also recognized him as the same man who often passed by our house on the way to the police or gendarmerie headquarters—to all appearances to make denunciations. He said, "I have a letter from Mr. Kazik," and he pulled out a rather fat envelope from under his homespun cloth jacket.

At first I thought that Kazik really had sent me a letter. I remained cautious, though, and asked with surprise, "Who is Kazik?"

He replied something indistinct. I opened the envelope and saw that in addition to a letter, there were some leaflets dropped from Soviet airplanes and a copy of the "Dawn," that was three weeks old. It struck me as strange that Kazik would send me Soviet leaflets in several copies when the Soviets were the enemies of Poland. *Whom would I distribute them to and why?* I also noticed at once that the date on the "Dawn" was old. Kazik wouldn't have added an old newspaper to a risky missive. The letter's contents also raised my suspicions. He asked, for example, about the number of police in Horodyszcze and requested that I examine the town's fortifications.

The letter began with an appeal for me to contribute to the struggle for independence. I quickly analyzed the letter. First of all, Kazik would have never sent such a letter with this peasant, nor would he appeal to my patriotism—this was not his style. He knew me well enough to realize that I would do whatever I could anyhow. Calls to patriotism were completely out of place here. As for the fortifications and the number of police in Horodyszcze, they were known by all of us in the forestry office as well as by everyone in the radius of many kilometers from Horodyszcze. The whole combination was out of the question as a letter from Kazik. Either the Gestapo had very poor advisers, or the person who took part in the composition of this letter did everything possible to warn me that it was a trap—perhaps the person was himself a member of the underground? This affair was a thinly disguised attempt to play with the feelings of a young—and perhaps naïve—Polish patriot. Those who had fabricated this letter believed that, spurred by the opening, I would write a reply to Kazik. Just that in itself would be like signing a death sentence for my family.

I began to act in front of the peasant because I was sure that they would ask him about my reaction to the letter. So I started to shout, "Idiots! Idiots! You can kiss my ass!" In the meantime Mother came home. I grabbed a pencil from the table and added at the bottom of the letter: "Potsaluyte mnie v sraku" (in Belorussian, it means, "Kiss my ass"). I wrote it in capital letters to stress it. I had to introduce Mother into this entire performance. I could tell that she was going through a lot, but her face did not show it.

"I will take this letter at once to the commandant of the battalion," said Mother, after I convinced her that the letter was a fake. "Come with me," she said to the peasant. The peasant went calmly, which was yet another proof of the falsity of the letter because just to have delivered such a letter from the partisans was sufficient to earn one a bullet in the head.

I waited for a long time for Mother's return. She told me that the mere fact that we had received such a letter was enough to have her arrested. The German had the letter, along with my addition, copied by his translator. Perhaps the addition caused the enemy to think of me as a silly, immature boy and hence someone who could not be dangerous. When Mother was leaving, the German said that if any further letters arrived, they should be delivered to his hands. "But of course," said Mother and left. The mounted S.D. police from Koldyczew led all the prisoners to their concentration camp. We interpreted that as the end of arrests, although now and then they happened again, but on a lesser scale.

At that time, my little sister came down with measles. Dr. Rowinska, who came to treat her, not only didn't accept any payment for the visit, but even brought us honey and butter, which helped us greatly. Then it was my turn to be sick. I had a high fever and was delirious. I thought that now we were helpless toward the Germans. Only God could save us. The axe which I placed next to my bed at all times was now without a master. I always had the following plan: when they'd come to arrest us, I would kill the first person entering the room with the axe. Then I'd kill all the others with his gun, and then we would run away. In my illness, my imagination worked intensely, and I kept killing Germans, Ukrainians, Bobkos, and Winogradows, for we were living separated by only a thin wall from the people who could annihilate us at any moment.

Old Mrs. Winogradowa was living the happiest days of her life. Her two sons brought home various things from the houses of the arrested Poles. As the Germans were arresting entire families, all their possessions were being liquidated. Much of that property was the post-Jewish goods that those people had pilfered a few years earlier. Micha Winogradow led the action of liquidating the post-Polish property. In his room, I saw many objects that had previously belonged to his good friend, the Pole Gruszyn, now arrested. We knew that they wouldn't become rich by taking over our property, and they (the Winogradows and others) knew that as well, so that would not be a reason to arrest us. We also suspected that as our neighbors, they may have been afraid that we knew about their doings, and that was why they did not denounce us—they might even have shielded us against arrest.

I was almost recovered when Dr. Piaskowski, as the doctor for the region, ordered that a large sign be put on the house: "Contagious disease: Do Not Enter." When Mrs. Winogradowa heard this, she made a big scene. "What! Such a sign on my house? Get up! There's nothing wrong with you!" It wasn't a good idea to contradict her, because, with her two sons, she was now mistress of our life and death, but Mother managed to appease her somehow. We didn't put up the sign.

New arrests did not spare even those who sucked up to the Germans the most. Mrs. Lechowa—one of the richest inhabitants of Horodyszcze and the owner of the butcher shop—who organized fancy receptions for the Germans and wined and dined them, was among those arrested, along with her son. Dr. Piaskowski also shared the fate of the other Poles, even though he entertained all the German gendarmes such as Reines and Gustaw, the executioners of innocent, helpless people. The Germans no longer trusted many of their "friends," especially the ones who sucked up to them the most. As for us, everybody knew that we were a poor family and that no Germans ever came to our house because we never invited anyone. It's possible that we weren't perceived as dangerous.

I remember very clearly the moment that was most critical for us during those arrests. Through the window, I saw a group of armed men going by our house. They're going to arrest someone. We were terrified again; they could stop to pick us up on their way back. This time we were all at home. We could hear the steps of the returning men. They were coming closer and closer. Now they were by our house. They stopped. My heart beat loudly. I heard someone say, "It's here."

My little sister was crying softly. God saved us that time as well. Mother, who was standing behind the curtain, told us later that those were Germans with Bobko and Misha Winogradow. Bobko waved his hat as if to say that it wasn't necessary, and Misha immediately agreed and also made a gesture that signified, "Let's leave them alone."

For the second time, the new batch of prisoners was to be transported to Koldyczewo. For the purpose, the Germans confiscated a number of wagons from nearby villages. Right next to our house stood the wagon with Mrs. Piaskowska and her two little sons. She was arrested soon after her husband's arrest. In front of us was the woman who, we believed, had told Reines that we were Jews and who pretended so hard to be a fervent Catholic. "We don't have to wear medallions," her two sons had said to my sister on some occasion. This created a very different picture of Mrs. Piaskowska in our minds because it meant that at home they discussed who should wear a medallion and who shouldn't. Mrs. Piaskowska wore one because she looked a lot like a Jewess. Dr. Rowinska, too, claimed that Piaskowska was Jewish, but she said it to us in greatest confidence. Not everyone was an informant. Piaskowska and her two little boys were crying terribly, while the other prisoners were very calm. We didn't dare approach the window for fear that she might see us. She could try to "rehabilitate" herself at the last minute at our expense. So we continued to watch the scene on the sly. I could see that the arrested young men had their hands tied behind them, and some of them still wore their Polish military four-cornered caps.

Even after this second transport to Koldyczewo, the arrests still continued. Every Monday, there were new victims, which meant that our nerves were perpetually tense. Soon that terrible wave passed. We were now part of a very small group of Poles who had survived. Other than the three of us, there were the priest's housekeeper and her young daughter, Dr. Rowinska with her daughter and husband, the photographer Matuszczak, the old Mrs. Pietraszycka and her son. (One of her imprisoned daughters had worked with Mother in the Rayonova Uprava as a typist and, as I already mentioned, had been on very good terms with my mother.)

A great bombardment east of Baranowicze stirred us up a bit. The sky was covered with a glow; beautiful, Christmas-tree-like rocket flames blossomed one after another, and the buzzing of airplanes resounded like music. It was very hard to disguise our joy. The bombardment lasted half an hour and gave us courage and strength to keep on going. The Winogradows moved about nervously and attempted to ignore it. "Oh, it's nothing," they kept saying. The afterglow lasted a long time and reminded us that there were forces countering the murderers and that these forces were coming closer. The peasants said that, with an ear to the ground, it was possible to hear the artillery clearly. I refused to believe this because it was too good to be true. A month after that memorable bombardment, we heard a distant cannonade. This time there was no need to put an ear to the ground. I listened to the sounds of gunfire every day. I had excellent ears; I could distinguish distant explosions before anyone else could hear them. I told Mother and my little sister about it. They tried to listen, but they couldn't hear anything. Then the sounds came closer and became audible to everyone. I thought that these were the sounds of the Germans fighting the partisans on a greater scale.

A few days later, a transport train came through the town going west. I stood by the window in a darkened room and watched as one cart followed another west. *Was it possible that the Germans were indeed retreating?* After our recent experiences, I was in such a state of nervous prostration that I could not even process the thought that the Germans could be retreating—it seemed abnormal. I was still standing by the window when a passing German soldier made a threatening gesture in my direction. Apparently he had noticed my silhouette against the window. He could have shot at me as well, so I moved away.

A few days passed in an atmosphere of pleasant agitation. We barely slept at night because Soviet airplanes passed over the town all the time. The rotating reflector that the Germans had installed a long while back seemed to attract them. Once, a plane flew low, and we heard a burst of shots from a machine gun aimed at the town. We derived great satisfaction from seeing how downcast our enemies were. The first few bombs and the fire of a house caused by a missile chased people out of Horodyszcze. In the evenings, people left the town to spend the night in neighboring villages. It was grand to watch the bombardment of Baranowicze. At last, justice was falling from the sky onto this seat of merciless power, violence, and murder. I enjoyed lying in the garden because, being outside, I could delight all the more in the sight of the glow in the sky. It was so cold that I couldn't sleep, but I felt wonderful.

One day, when I came back from the timber yard, Mother was unexpectedly home. She started kissing me and calling, *"They've announced the evacuation!"* I showed no emotion and listened to her without saying anything. "I can see you don't believe me," Mother said. "Go see for yourself how they're burning official papers." I walked out into the street. Indeed, in front of all the offices, there were piles of burning papers. It was incredible. The Germans announced that everyone must be evacuated.

First to go were the police with the civilians, and then Zigling's battalion. Once I accepted the evacuation as a fact, I decided to remain behind. We would hide somewhere in the country side and wait there for the liberation. On the other hand, however, we felt an irrepressible urge to leave this town where we had gone through so much. The Germans claimed that they were going toward Warsaw or even to Warsaw. That would have been very convenient for us because we could hope to meet some of our relatives there. After all, once this area was liberated, Warsaw would be next, we thought. Another motivating factor was that the Germans were supposedly leaving in their wake a desert and a cemetery. That was what the German soldiers returning from the front said, *"Alles kaput!"*

At last, the fever of departing engulfed everyone. The priest's housekeeper, a very bright woman, also claimed that we must go because the Germans would "club everyone to death" before leaving—everyone, meaning all the remaining Poles. The possibility of leaving behind this hell of constant anxiety inspired everyone. Someone brought the news that in Koldyczewo, all the prisoners had been shot to death. Mrs. Pietraszycka, whose husband had been taken to Siberia long before and whose two daughters and one son had been arrested recently, lamented loudly in the streets and looked for a cart on which to leave. It was a kind of collective insanity, this drive to leave.

We didn't have a cart, so we seated ourselves on a police wagon drawn by a very large horse. I was supposed to drive. I had never before had anything to do with such a large beast, and here I was the driver of a wagon filled to overflowing with ammunition. There was a heavy machine gun on top, but I had no idea what was hidden underneath the straw. The wagons followed each other in a line. I don't know how on earth I managed to drive down the hill without running into the wagon in front of me. At the last moment, I was able to turn in such a way that my horse landed next to the wagon in front. This gave me hope that I would cope with my new role. Soon there was another hill, and this time I managed well. The wagon behind capsized, and boxes with ammunition spilled all over the road. This encouraged me further. Soon Horodyszcze was behind us. We were among a long line of wagons loaded to the brim. Having burned many things at the time of greatest threat, we had very few personal belongings: they all fit in a small sack and in a couple of baskets with provisions. We passed through villages and crossed fields. In one of the villages, the Germans noticed a horse tied to a tree and an empty wagon next to it. They took both at once and gave them to us, wanting to get rid of the few civilians who were still on their wagons. First, however, they transferred the load from the police wagon to ours, but without giving us the machine gun and the ammunition.

I was now the owner of a wagon, which gave me more freedom of movement. I still couldn't tell what was under the straw. The new wagon became our home on wheels. We slept in it and ate in it. We passed through rich estates and villages. Fields and meadows abounded in freshly cut feed for the horses, so the animals had enough to eat. I felt very different than in Horodyszcze. All at once, we were free of so many worries and cares. It seemed that we were safe—after all, no one would bother to denounce people or to arrest them in the middle of running away! It had been years since we last felt so happy. I became a normal man. We were going in the direction of home, in the direction of the city of Lodz. We knew we would be liberated soon. We had enough food—I had stolen delicious canned meat and other foods from the policemen. We had a great appetite. The Germans added to our load several sacks with sweaters. They claimed that our horse was strong and that it could pull more than others, which was true. The horse was young, of a pretty gray color, and pulled the wagon without any effort.

We passed through large virgin forests. At night, it wasn't very pleasant. It was so dark that walking next to the wagon, I ran into trees. Slonim was already behind us. We were now following an asphalt road, and during the day the heat was unbearable. The fatigue overwhelmed me. Cars passing next to us were practically rubbing against our wagon. An accident could happen any minute. I was seeing red circles in front of my eyes from exhaustion. We had no drinking water, so in order to get a drink, I had to jump off the wagon, run to a roadside spring, take a few gulps, and then run after my wagon to catch up with it. We were not allowed to stop or turn anywhere. To make things worse, the rims of the wheels began to slip off because of the great heat, which dried out the wood. I watched the wheels anxiously, and at every opportunity, I tried to adjust them. At last, we arrived in some village for a two-day halt. I drove the wagon into a little pond, and there the water did its job: the rims were once again firmly set on the wheels.

Farther on, the Belorussian policemen began to disappear. At one stopping place, two would be gone, at another, three, and so on. The number of wagons traveling with us also diminished. I thought that it made little sense to escape now when we were closer and closer to home. The Germans were still saying that we were going toward Warsaw, and the direction seemed right. But soon it became apparent to me that as we kept moving, we were deviating too much to the north, and I was sure of that when we crossed the Grodno-Bialystok road. So the Germans were lying, and, in reality, we were going not to Warsaw, but to East Prussia. At the command of the main German officer, we now had to be the fourth wagon in line at all times. *Did they suspect that we wanted to get away?* There was nothing to do about it, and so we drove as the fourth wagon. This reminded me that we were still in the power of the "supermen." It was obvious that the arrival in East Prussia would end tragically for us. They would take me at once to forced labor, and there would be a medical examination … We had to run away at all costs.

I shared these thoughts with Mother and wanted to put my plan into action at once. Mother did not agree. "It's certain death! They can see us from the front and from behind. Let's stay! We'll see farther on." I decided to brace myself. The escape was imperative, and Mother couldn't accept that. This time, I would not listen to my mother, I decided.

We stopped briefly in the village of Sokolany. Near our camp there was a large church. Something told me to go to the church and ask the priest how and where to escape. I introduced myself as a Warsaw native eager to get back to Warsaw. I told the priest that the Germans were headed to East Prussia, and that was why I had to escape and wait until the front passes.

The priest approved of my plan and even encouraged me, "You must run away." Then he gave me a plan: "Half a kilometer from here, the road goes uphill. Before the hill, there is a cross on the left hand side, and right near there, there is a little side road. You must turn left there and reach the village of Kozi Lug. Then, go straight to the village administrator and tell him that I sent you. You be assured that he will welcome you, and you'll be able to stay there until the front is gone." The priest wrote down for me the name of the village and the last name of the village administrator.

"But how can I get away when I'm guarded both in front and from behind?"

"Stay calm," he said. "Turn where I've told you, and you'll see that they won't even notice." I thanked the priest. I knew that I must turn at the cross at all cost. This was our only chance. I heard the Germans' whistles announcing the departure. Horses were being harnessed. I thought quickly. *I'll try to ride last, and in this way, it'll be easier for me to escape unnoticed.* Two cars with gendarmes had entered the road already, and the wagons followed suit. I took as long as possible harnessing my horse, and so entering the road, I was already in the second half of the column, and not where I was supposed to be, fourth in line. After a few minutes, I drove a bit off the road and stopped. I began to adjust the harness. I tied and untied the horse-collar and then reentered the column. This time mine was the fifth wagon from the end. In the distance, I could distinguish the hill and next to it clearly the cross. *That's where I have to turn,* I thought. I had to be last at all cost. Again, I repeated my maneuver with the horse-collar. I felt the wagons passing me by, one by one, until at last the car with the gendarmes went by as well. But then, all of a sudden, a mounted policeman appeared next to us. I had no choice but to move on. Between my wagon and the last wagon of the column, there was about a one-hundred-meter distance. We reached the place where I was supposed to turn off the road. Nearby, there was a large German camp. The policeman was not leaving our side. With an aching heart, I passed by the cross and began the climb up hill. The other wagons were no longer in sight because they had already driven down the other side of the hill. I drove as slowly as I possibly could, and soon the distance between us and the policeman on horseback increased. In the meantime, perhaps from the extreme heat and fatigue, the policeman appeared to have forgotten about us. Another moment and he was out of our sight as well. I was halfway up the mountain by now. Without giving it another thought, I turned around.

A few minutes later, I was at the foot of the hill. The road by the cross was ahead of me. I took it, and I kept driving as fast as I could. Our horse seemed to understand the situation and began to gallop. I prayed to God—that he would save us, that the Germans from our column wouldn't notice our absence, and that the Germans from the nearby camp wouldn't become interested in us. I saw a forest not far from us. *Oh, to get there, to get there! There we'll be able to hide.* Very far off, I saw two riders who seemed to be approaching. We were rushing ahead. The German camp remained far behind. At last, we entered the forest. The sun set and the night was reigning in the world. We were now driving at a walking pace, and we felt like free people who had just escaped from Hitler's power. It was quiet and blissful. We passed single houses. I had to knock on one of the doors to ask for the village administrator. Soon we were in front of his house.

We gave the little piece of paper on which the priest had written the name of the village and the administrator's name to the administrator as a kind of written recommendation from the priest. This had an immediate effect, and we were very well received. We ate a copious supper and fell asleep at once. The following day, the village administrator told us that we would sleep at the neighbors. We had with us two sacks of new German sweaters that the Germans had loaded onto our cart during the evacuation, and we decided to exchange them for food. We also had woolen army blankets, and under the straw, I could feel some guns and who knows what else. I was desperate for work, and I offered to tend cattle. I followed a herd of cows on my gray horse, bare-back. The forest was never-ending. I was on the edge of the Bialowieza Forest. There were lots of wild strawberries, blueberries, and raspberries there. I had never before seen such a forest.

One evening, I was watching the glow in the sky. Every evening there was a glow, and the sound of bombardments was incessant. I felt that I was close to the finish line, close to complete salvation: the arrival of the Red Army. A girl, the young and shapely daughter of our host, stood next to me. All the dams, all the obstacles I put in the way of "sinful thoughts," and especially deeds, burst at that moment. I took the girl by the waist, and soon I was asking her whether she would come with me to the barn.

She answered that it was obvious I was a "city boy" because I was so bold, and apparently she liked that because she made a gesture that meant "yes." But here, louder explosions cooled my blood off and reminded me I still needed much grace from God to survive the front. So I couldn't sin.

The following day, I was tending the herd when I heard a loud noise coming from the road. I chased the cows into the forest, and I hid even deeper. When I returned home with the cows, Mother met me with a very sad face. You know what happened?" she asked. "We have nothing left. Ukrainians came and found our things in the barn. First they found the German sweaters and the guns, and they asked who they belonged to. I hid in the rye because, otherwise, they would have killed me."

I knew that among our things there was the bit of jewelry that we had miraculously saved. "All of that is nothing compared to the fact that we are alive," I said. I wasn't only trying to console Mother; I actually wasn't too concerned. Those jewels could have been lost so many times already that it wasn't a reason to cry.

We were standing next to the barn when our host came out of the barn, carrying the basket with our things. "They left this," he said. "I found it under the straw." That was the basket with the jewelry! It also turned out that the Ukrainians took the neighbors' cows, which were grazing in the woods next to the road. Our host was very glad that I had saved his cows. Since we had nothing with which to pay for our food, except for the sweaters which we wanted to keep for future expenses, we moved back to the village administrator's house. In exchange for his hospitality, we gave him our gray horse, which we couldn't really use anyhow.

Many paths crossed the forest. One day, I was riding with the village administrator's farmhand when, just before we came to a path, I heard the roar of an engine. There was no time to lose; after all, they could mistake us for partisans or shoot us for sport. It was too late to turn back, especially as the forest here was not very dense. We crossed the path in a flash and barely had enough time to hide in the thicket before the arrival of a car filled with German soldiers. It was hard to believe they hadn't seen us. *Had the Germans changed?*

The front was closer and closer. We decided to build a strong shelter. I reinforced the potato cellar with beams and added boards on top that I then covered with dirt. Our host did not give me the wood willingly, and I took some of it while he wasn't looking. In addition to this reinforcement, I dug, with the help of the farmhand, a zigzag trench, just in case. All this, I camouflaged with branches. The cellar was rather large, and that was where we spent the nights. The planes kept circling continuously and low, dropping rockets. I would have preferred to sleep in the barn, but for my mother's sake I would go to the cellar.

One morning, two tractors arrived, pulling behind them German artillery cannons. The gun barrels were aimed east, and the bombardment began. The front had caught up with us. The explosions were so loud that we no longer heard one another. We hid in our bunker. In the evening, the gunfire quieted down, and the women went to get some food. I awaited my mother's return with impatience. She came back soon with hot soup. The Germans in the unit stationed next to us didn't show any hostility toward us; either this was their new policy during the retreat, or we were simply lucky.

Two days later, five more cannons similar to the ones that were already next to us were brought in. The bombardment that began was pure hell. Dirt fell on our heads. During a short interval in the gunfire, the women again went to get food, while the men tried to stay out of the Germans' sight. I was sitting on the threshold of the bunker when I heard a sudden whiz, then another one, and then I saw that the sand on the edge of the forest had risen into the air. This was the "flight" of the Soviet missiles, some fifty yards from us. The house was between us and the forest, and Mother was there. I was terrified. What could I do? *Ah, may Mother come back now! Why did she leave at all?* The minutes of her absence seemed to last an infinity. I prayed that she might return before the next series of missiles. Dear, beloved Mother came in the end and brought hot soup. I promised myself not to let her out of the shelter again, even if there was nothing to eat.

The Germans renewed their bombardment. The unit consisted mainly of Russians. Once, I saw the German corporal beat one of his subordinate Russian soldiers in a horrible manner. The blood of the victim flowed freely, but the German continued the beating. One of those Russians often came to see us in the bunker. He brought us things that he took from the supply wagon. I got a pair of socks from him. He wanted to escape the Germans very badly, but he was afraid. He said he hated them and that they had taken him into the army by force in the Caucasus. He gave us advice on how to protect ourselves from artillery fire and generally was very nice. His name was Volodya.

On the fourth day after the arrival of the German battery, we suddenly heard a second-long whiz and a great explosion. Soon it happened again. Screams and chaos were everywhere. Volodya had just enough time to jump into our bunker, and then a series of explosions resounded, one after the other, closer and closer to us. I prayed for God to save us.

Suddenly, rushing air and the smoke of burned gunpowder filled our shelter, and a great explosion threw us to the ground. Sand was falling on our heads. The shell must have hit very nearby. When things calmed down a bit, I wanted to look out to see what was going on outside, but they wouldn't let me. Everyone was still trembling with fear. Volodya disappeared, God knows when. Soon, however, he returned and told us that the missiles had hit the nearby hut, which had been put hastily together with wooden boards. The Germans had been inside playing cards; now one was dead, the other gravely wounded. I thought of the boards that the village administrator begrudged us so. In the meantime, everything became quiet outside. Both sides were silent, but, nonetheless, we were afraid to leave the bunker. Taking advantage of a moment when everyone was taking a nap, I put my head out to see what was happening. There was no one in the yard and in the area.

The Germans had been swept away. The Soviet shells had their effect. It would make sense if the artillery was followed by the infantry, that is, the first line of the front. We did not think they would put up a defense in the forest. The Germans were afraid of the forests in the east because of the partisans, so we decided to hide in the forest.

Together with a family from Sokolka who also had escaped the bombardment, we quickly crossed the few hundred meters dividing us from the forest. The village administrator had let all his cattle into the forest and even constructed a provisional enclosure for pigs and piglets. We spent our first night in the forest underneath a tree. It was calm and quiet.

The following day, we had no more food, but the tension and the stress made us oblivious to our hunger. We were, however, terribly thirsty. At dinnertime, we heard the first gun shots. It was clear that the first front line was fast approaching, and we had to find a shelter from the artillery and the bullets. Quite deeply in the forest, there was a clearing and a pile of raw, unhewn wood. The wood was stored in layers, while next to the ground there were only two logs. We slipped underneath one of the piles. This was a good shelter; it could protect us from bullets and even from grenades. The roof was made of three layers of wet wood. It was, however, impossible to lie there a long time because one could not stand up. Now and then we crawled out, but Mother and my little sister soon crawled back in there. Large fires marked the contour of the forest. I was convinced that the Germans were burning houses during their retreat and that the village administrator's house was also consumed by fire. Small, nimble planes dived in the areas of the fire and were immediately shot at, which I could see by the appearance of many small white clouds in the sky.

Our little group began reciting the prayer to St. Mary. It was picturesque and threatening at once: this prayer in the beautiful old forest against the backdrop of a raging fire and the clouds of smoke. When the prayer was about half done, we heard a short whiz and an explosion. A grenade fell nearby. In the blink of an eye, we were all flat on the ground in our hiding place. Missiles flew over the forest constantly now. *Vioooo, vioooo* was heard every moment. We spent the night underneath the wood.

In the morning, we were unbearably thirsty. I put leaves of the nearby bushes in my mouth as they were wet with dew. Soon everyone started imitating me. There were lots of raspberries growing there, and their fruit was our only food. In the afternoon, we returned to our shelter because we heard numerous steps. A group of seven Germans passed just next to us. We saw only their boots. It was a miracle that they didn't see us, especially since our things lay hidden right next to the path on which they walked. After this incident, we were afraid to show our heads. Thirst and hunger tortured us. During the night, German columns and lots of infantry passed close to us. It would have been enough for one of the Germans to use a flashlight in order to discover us. I did not know then that those were the last retreating Germans.

When morning came, I made a quick trip to pick some raspberries for Mother and my little sister. I was so preoccupied with picking the berries that I was completely oblivious to what was going on around me.

"Podaydite tut, podaydite blize (come here; come closer)," I heard suddenly. I turned toward the voice and saw two soldiers: one on a horse, the other with a bicycle. At first I thought these were "Vlasovtsy" (Russians commanded by Vlasov who were fighting on the side of the Germans), and for a moment I hesitated, but an escape was impossible; they were armed.

It would be too good to be true if these were Soviet soldiers, I said to myself. I walked up closer to them. I could see their epaulettes and remembered that the German newspapers wrote that the Red Army had introduced epaulettes. Then I noticed a small red star on the cap of one of the soldiers. "Tovarishche, vy russkiye, sovietskye (friends, you are Russian, Soviets)," I cried.

"Da," they answered. "Podazdite, tam yesche toze nahoditsya ludie katorye vas izdayut (wait; there are people there who are waiting for you)." I presented them with all the raspberries that I had collected and ran as fast as I could to our hiding place.

"They've liberated us!" I screamed. ""They've liberated us! Come quickly! They're here!" Speedily I ran back to *them*. I began hugging and touching them to make sure they were indeed real. Mother and my little sister were laughing, and Mother had tears in her eyes. We thanked them for having freed us. The Russians asked us not to forget them. They gave us their field post address. Their names were:

ZDANOV AND MADZIANOV.

I shall never forget these soldiers.

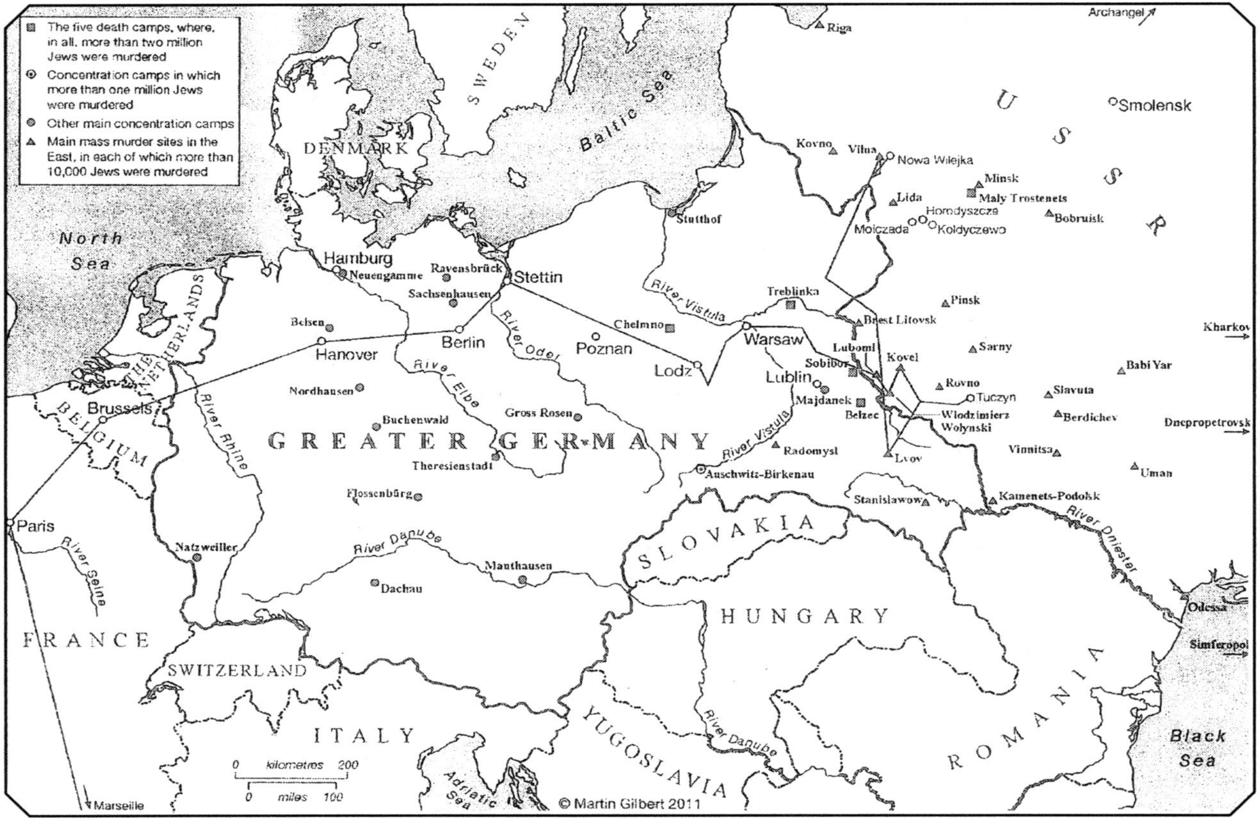
The five death camps, where, in all, more than two million Jews were murdered
Concentration camps in which more than one million Jews were murdered
Other main concentration camps
Main mass murder sites in the East, in each of which more than 10,000 Jews were murdered
North Sea
Baltic Sea
SWEDEN
DENMARK
THE NETHERLANDS
BELGIUM
FRANCE
SWITZERLAND
ITALY
GREATER GERMANY
SLOVAKIA
HUNGARY
YUGOSLAVIA
ROMANIA
USSR
Black Sea
Adriatic Sea
Hamburg
Neuengamme
Ravensbrück
Sachsenhausen
Stettin
Stutthof
Belsen
Hanover
Berlin
Poznan
Chelmno
Lodz
Treblinka
Warsaw
Lublin
Sobibor
Majdanek
Belzec
Luboml
Brest Litovsk
Kovel
Nordhausen
Buchenwald
Gross Rosen
Theresienstadt
Flossenbürg
Natzweiler
Dachau
Mauthausen
Auschwitz-Birkenau
Radomysl
Brussels
Paris
Marseille
River Seine
River Rhine
River Elbe
River Oder
River Vistula
River Danube
River Dniester
Riga
Kovno
Vilna
Nowa Wilejka
Lida
Minsk
Maly Trostenets
Horodyszcze
Molczada
Koldyczewo
Bobruisk
Smolensk
Archangel
Pinsk
Sarny
Rovno
Tuczyn
Wlodzimierz Wolynski
Lvov
Stanislawow
Kamenets-Podolsk
Vinnitsa
Slavuta
Berdichev
Babi Yar
Uman
Kharkov
Dnepropetrovsk
Odessa
Simferopol
0 kilometres 200
0 miles 100
© Martin Gilbert 2011

CHAPTER NINE

WE SET OUT ON our return—the way to life. We wanted to find life. We wanted to find the ideal that would make life worth living. We wanted our sufferings to be redeemed by the lightness of the life to come. We thought that, as Jews, we would be a rarity and that people would pay us homage. Life was smiling at us. Entire battalions were passing next to us. One officer asked which way the Germans had run away. Unfortunately, we couldn't tell him, since we had not seen which way they had turned—next to our hiding place, there was a fork in the road.

We finally made it back to the village administrator's house. The house was there, but the walls bore bullet marks. The barn, on the other hand, was half burned, and there were two dead German horses in it. In the yard, there were boxes and boxes of cartridge shells. The Germans collected empty shells up to the last minute. Our host was scrupulously collecting and carrying home German leather bags, ebonite soap boxes, and anything else that was of value. The family from Sokolka decided to return to their home town at once. They invited us to stay with them, asking us to wait at their place until Warsaw was free. They thought it would happen soon.

We decided, though, to remain at the village administrator's to rest a bit and perhaps to help him with the harvest. We were now free and able to decide on our own what to do with our life. It was a real pleasure to watch the Soviet cars drive by on the high road. We saw it as a certain guarantee of security. The phone technicians installed a telephone in the kitchen, and every few minutes we could hear them call, "Hallo Nakoneczna, hallo Nakoneczna." And so on—for two days and nights. Then they went on.

A few days later, we, too, left the village administrator's house. Our will to use our new freedom to move drove us on. We were free and, therefore, could go wherever we pleased. It was wonderful. We took our remaining possessions and some provisions for the trip, and we walked up to the high road.

The first Soviet car going by stopped. "Tovarishch, podvizite nas (Comrade, please give us a ride)," said Mother.

"Vlizayte (hop in)," said the driver.

We rode for the first time in years as free people in a free car. Our host's dog, which had gotten very attached to us, followed the car for a long time, until at last his forces gave out, and he stopped.

We were approaching Sokolka. After a short drive, we found ourselves in a ruined town. The family that we had met during the front received us very warmly, according to the principle of Polish hospitality "czym chata bogata, tym rada" (what's in the house is for the guests), but there wasn't much in the house, and after the first day, there was nothing. The owners of vegetable gardens wouldn't even sell us potatoes because they claimed not to know their price. The same was true for milk and bread. We barely managed to get some food on credit, and we were supposed to pay for it when the prices became known. As a result, we only ate enough not to starve. I was hungry all day long. We admired the generosity of these people who shared everything with us and apologized to us that there was so little food. Many years later, we tried to find this family from Sokolka to do something for them in return, but they no longer lived there and had left no forwarding address.

We decided to go to the town commandant and tell him that we were Jewish. We were convinced that the officials would give us and our hosts some provisions and everything we might need. Why not use the fact that we were Jews who had escaped destruction? We believed that it would open new possibilities for us. We went to look for the commandant of the town. Suddenly, we noticed a Jewish family. They were walking, suitcases in hand, and next to them walked two Soviet soldiers who were helping them carry something. I don't know why we didn't walk up to them. They were the first Jews we had seen since liberation. They were very frail, but their faces were beaming. Our hearts went out to them, but still we did not walk up to them. We were not yet at ease, even though there was nothing to fear any longer. Every day the newspapers informed of dozens of liberated towns, but there was no mention of Warsaw. We did find out from another source that an uprising had erupted there and that the "London government" (the anti-communist Polish government in exile) had taken power there.

We never found the commandant of the town of Sokolka, but, quite by accident, we ran into Dr. Rowinska and her daughter, who had ended up there from Horodyszcze. We did not reveal our true origin to her either, even though once we had dreamed of the day when we would tell the whole world that we were Jewish. Subconscious fear was still deeply embedded in us.

After a three-week stay in Sokolka, we decided to go to Wilno, hoping to find out something about Father there. We expected that there might be news from him there or some inquiry about us; after all, that was where he would be looking for us since Wilno was the last address he had. Moreover, we had left seven leather suitcases filled with clothes with the Krupowicz family. Our current clothes were rags, and we could really use new ones. Our desire to travel was so great that we left the very same day that we thought of it. It was so easy, so simple, and so convenient to travel!

"Tovarishch, podvizite nas (Comrade, please give us a ride)," Mother would say.

"Vlizayte (hop in)," was usually the reply, and presently we were on the road.

The family with whom we had stayed in Sokolka parted with us very cordially. They asked us to stay there and to open a café or a confectioner's. They gave us some pork fat for the road, which they must have bought on credit. We were moved by their conduct. Those were, indeed, excellent people. We left for Wilno without a single ruble to our name. The one ruble I had had in my pocket, I had given to a poor man in Sokolka.

We did have bread and pork fat—and that was plenty. *Once in Wilno we'll have time to worry further,* we thought. We crossed the new Polish-Soviet border in Kuznica and then headed straight to Grodno, where the car was going to stop. I thought of our good fortune in having met such decent people in Sokolka. From what they told us and from the great numbers of young people in the streets, it seemed that the inhabitants of the town (except for Jews) had not suffered during the German occupation; they had led peaceful lives.

When we reached Grodno, Mother decided to go to the city commandant and ask for further transportation. For the time being, we went to the nearest apartment and asked to be allowed to wash up and rest. The owners agreed at once, much in the style of Polish hospitality, and even made us some hot tea. We had great luck with people. I waited impatiently for Mother to return from the Grodno commandant. There was no need to be nervous the way I had been in Horodyszcze or in Baranowicze. I expected only a pleasant surprise. In my imagination, we would be cared for and given food and a place to rest, and then the officials would facilitate our journey. But my imagination was wrong. The city commandant paid no attention to Mother's declaration that she was Jewish. We could count only on ourselves. There seemed to be no car going to Wilno.

At last, a truck carrying gasoline in barrels stopped. This time, the driver agreed to give us a lift without much enthusiasm. We were on a side road when the driver told us, in a very rude manner, to get out. Mother started to plead with him to let us continue. We were in a field, and it would have been impossible to find another ride there. The driver kept insisting that we get off. That was when Mother used her trump card: "Ya Yevrieyka (I'm Jewish)." But this had the opposite effect from the one intended. "Seyczas zlezat (get off at once)!" shouted the driver, but faced with our unwillingness to move, after a ten-minute argument, he uttered a curse and drove on. Several women soldiers sitting on the truck smiled maliciously during the entire scene, but did not say a word. This convinced us that we should not boast too much of our origin.

We arrived in Lida. Life was thriving there; we could see that, above all, at the marketplace. One could freely buy and sell produce. We walked around the market for the pleasure of looking at things; we had not been to a market in over three years—but we didn't have even a kopeck (the smallest unit of Russian currency). People were selling delicious apples; we hadn't eaten apples like that in years. Mother, with her practical mind, took a nickel-plated spoon out of our basket and sold it to a peddler. We got thirty rubles for it and at once bought two kilograms of apples: life was good.

At last, we also found the right truck. We rode to Wilno with a merry group of officers. They were singing the entire time, which made the trip very pleasant. Just before we got to the city, they advised us to get off because at night Wilno was usually bombed. Many people had been killed in the last bombing. We had no idea if we'd find someone we knew and a place to sleep, so, in any case, we decided to spend the night nearby and enter the city the following morning. We slept in a barn, along with many people who left the city at night to avoid the bombs. In the morning, we were at the city gates.

"Tovarishch, pozhousta vashe bumagi (Comrade, may I see your papers)?" the NKVD guard at the gate said to me.

"Vy z 28 goda, tak dolzhny poyti v armiu (you were born in 1928, so you are subject to the draft)."

In reality, I was born in 1925.

This was a surprise; we had no idea that there was a mobilization in Wilno.

"Vy tut ostanetes (you will stay here)," he said to me, "a vy mozhete poyti (and you can go)," he said to Mother and my little sister.

Now we're in trouble, I thought to myself. But we had to get out of this somehow. I told the guard that we had only now arrived and that I would report to the military commission on my own.

"In this case, I will take your information," he said, "and if anyone stops you further on, just tell them you are already signed up." We breathed a sigh of relief.

Nothing stood in our way; we could enter the city that we had left in 1941 as if running from the plague. We went first to 17 Zawalna St., where we had last lived. We found ourselves standing in front of the house where we had gone through so much and where our struggle for life in the times of Hitler's violence had begun. We wanted to see the janitor, a woman who had always been kind to us and with whom we were hoping to find a letter from Father. She greeted us with true joy, but she had no letter for us and no news. If he were alive, he'd surely try to communicate with us at this address, we thought. Therefore, the lack of a letter was very depressing. On the other hand, we were somewhat cheered up by the fact that the mail wasn't functioning regularly yet. Our apartment, like others in this house, had been taken over by a military hospital. We spent the night at the janitor's in the basement and decided to go to Bukiszki to reclaim our things in the morning.

Bukiszki was in front of us, but this time we didn't need to seek shelter there from the enemy. We approached Krupowiczes' farm. We wore the same clothes in which we had left three years earlier, the only difference being that they were shabby and patched. We could see the house where we had lived after leaving Wilno. In front of the barn were the small woods where I had asked God to save us. In a field by the road, I recognized Krupowicz and his wife, harvesting barley. Everything unchanged, just as it was then, I thought. Apparently they went through the war rather smoothly.

"God bless you!" I called out. Krupowiczowa looked at us for a moment, stopped working (I bet her heart stopped beating as well), and then, as if nothing had happened, continued her work. Krupowicz, on the other hand, smiled and walked up to meet us.

"God bless!" I called again, this time practically into Krupowiczowa's ear. She gave us a fake smile, and then she said, "Mother of God, it's you!" The second thing she said was, "Thank God you survived; that's what counts. Things are not so important."

It was obvious what she was alluding to, but I didn't want to get into this and worry about it while we had the tremendous satisfaction of showing her that *we were alive*, showing it to the people who were counting on never seeing us again. I understood that Krupowiczowa wanted to delay the consciousness of our arrival, and that was why at first, she pretended not to see or not to recognize us, even though we were standing right next to her. In any case, we had the satisfaction of being there.

Before we could reach the house, Krupowiczowa hastily recited the sentence that must have been ready for a while, "just in case.": "The Gestapo searched our house and took almost all of your things. I will look for what is left and give it back to you."

The Krupowiczes' daughters received us coldly. They didn't have enough manners to hide their hostility, the way their parents were doing it at the moment. Nonetheless, they made us very comfortable beds for the night. We slept on white sheets and had comforters in clean, embroidered duvets.

Mother recognized her own sheets, even though the monogramming had been removed. "These are our sheets," Mother said gently to Krupowiczowa.

"No, I bought this at the market in Wilno," answered Krupowiczowa.

In the morning, we awoke wonderfully refreshed. Krupowicz told us about the difficulties they had when their daughters were nearly deported, but thanks to the Lithuanians from the estate, they were spared. I remembered the dates these girls had had with the Lithuanians, and I understood in what manner they must have paid for this protection.

The first question we had for Krupowicz was "Where is Chigryn?" We concealed the fact that we knew well that Chigryn had made it as far as the Platers' because, according to the agreement, Krupowicz was supposed to keep Chigryn until the end of the war.

He told us that he had kept him in the barn, and then when winter came, he had taken him to the house; but when he saw that the war was lasting longer than expected, he had decided that it would be best if Chigryn was with us, that is, at the Platers' estate. His brother-in-law drove Chigryn to Lida, and from there he was supposed to go on.

We reminded him of the agreement. "I couldn't risk the lives of my entire family for one man," he answered.

We returned to Wilno with a suitcase of clothes, and Mother's astrakhan fur coat, considerably worse for the wear. It was clear that it had gotten much use in the Krupowicz family.

Upon arrival in Wilno, we decided to look for surviving relatives and friends. First of all, we went to the house of our aunt on Wielka Pohulanka Street, where we had originally stayed and where we had hidden during the Soviet deportations with the humpbacked Nastja. The exterior wall of the house was standing, but the rest of the house had burned. "Look, Mother. That's the stove from the room where I used to sleep!" I cried and pointed to a blackened stove that was practically hanging from the wall. We left that place with repugnance.

The large corner house on Poznanska Street where father's uncle Zlatin used to live seemed whole from a distance. But that was only an illusion; it was like a hollow tree that seems intact on the outside, but has been worm-eaten on the inside and can collapse at any moment. Other than the exterior walls, nothing remained. From there, we went to the apartment of my second aunt, on Nowogrodzka Street. The house was in one piece, but in the aunt's room lived complete strangers, and the janitor knew nothing of my aunt's fate.

Then we remembered the Kotlar family's house. We had no other relatives or friends. With trembling hands, we knocked on the door of 17 Weglowa Street, a small, one-story house, that was also connected with the story of our survival. A young man opened. Mother asked, "Is Ida here? Is she alive?"

He replied that Ida had escaped with Sioma to Russia, but Niuta was here. We were happy to find someone familiar at last. Niuta was one of the Kotlars' three daughters. She used to live in Olkienniki, and my sister stayed with her for a few weeks after Father had been deported to Russia. Niuta immediately invited us to stay with her, and we moved there the following day with our things.

Our first duty was to earn a living. Warsaw was not yet liberated, and for the time being, the border with Poland was closed, so we had no choice but to remain in Wilno. To have enough money to buy the bare necessities, we started by selling some of our things that we had reclaimed from the Krupowicz family, and we began to look for permanent employment. Niuta supported herself by working at a hospital, and she shared the house with a girlfriend. Hospital work was the best possible kind in those days because it enabled access to food. Through an officer who was Niuta's friend, Mother also got a job at the hospital. I didn't know exactly what kind of work this was because Mother didn't tell me what she was doing, and when I asked, she was evasive. But one day, when she came home with burns, it became evident that she did hard physical labor there, and the burns were a result of her carrying a cauldron of boiling water from one hospital yard to another. The food she brought home every evening, and which we awaited all day long, came from her own meal ration that she saved for us.

Soon thereafter, Mother stopped working at that hospital and moved to another one, where the conditions were much better and the work less strenuous. Finally, she managed to change jobs altogether: she found a position in the meteorological institute. This was clean, clerical work. In addition to a salary, once a week, she received "payok" (a food portion), which lasted us two days.

I had to find a job and find it fast.

The next step in our continuing efforts to find Father was to contact another one of his uncles who lived in Moscow. We didn't know his address, but we sent a letter to the address office. The reply came unexpectedly quickly, and enclosed with it, there was a money transfer for several hundred rubles. The knowledge that someone somewhere was thinking of us and wanted to help us cheered us up immensely. We received a very warm letter, in which our relatives assured us that they would undertake all possible efforts to find Father. But the mere fact that they knew nothing about Father's whereabouts diminished our hope for finding him. It seemed obvious to us that since he was in Russia, if he was alive, he would have contacted his uncle.

We were then all alone, but this realization hardened us all the more in our struggle for survival. While sending letters to Moscow, we asked the post office clerk whether she knew about some position for me. "I do happen to know," she said, "that in one of the bakeries they need an apprentice." She gave us the address. "Please come back, and let me know if you got the position. I'll be very glad to be able to help you. I'm guessing from the last name of the addressee on your letters that you are of Jewish origin, and I'm known here for helping Jews," she said, smiling kindly.

"I will bring you the first loaf of bread I bake," I said in response.

After many formalities, I began to work in the railway bakery. For the first time, I was going to taste, literally, my own hard-earned bread. My official salary came to one hundred rubles, for which I could buy one big can of tinned meat at the market. The true earnings came in the form of the additional loaves of bread, baked from the flour that we received for the entire batch.

Three people worked at the oven, and I was supposed to be their helper. We worked in three shifts: twelve hours of work, twenty-four hours of rest. Because of this, the shifts were sometimes at night and sometimes during the day. The nearest water well was on the other side of the street, in the yard of a house across from the bakery. It was a deep well, and it took a lot of turning of the pump handle to bring up a bucket of water. The bakery buckets were old and full of holes, so half of the water usually spilled on the way, even though we tried to block the holes with rags. I was completely exhausted and wet already after having brought just half of the water: thirty buckets. I couldn't rest, however, because I had to start mixing the dough, which was also hard work. The baker tossed the dough, and I had to knead it with my hands. When the dough was ready, I put the empty forms on a scale and filled them with dough, then carried them to a large table. There were 120 forms, and I had to work with great speed. Next, I placed the forms on a baker's shovel. The oven was bursting forth with unbearable heat, which I had to withstand until all the 120 forms were in. Then I would mix new dough and carefully take out the fresh, burning-hot bread so as not to break it, especially when the dough was delicate because it had been diluted. Greasing the forms was a kind of rest. I did this while sitting down because I could no longer stand up. All this work had to be repeated three times in the twelve hours. By the end of a shift, I was exhausted, but the tension—wondering how many loaves of bread I would get from the boss—kept me going. After my first day of work, I got one loaf, while my boss took seven and his two aides got six each. I was very proud of that loaf and took it home as a great triumph. We devoured it with an excellent appetite, forgetting my promise to the post office clerk.

My second shift happened to be at night. I fell asleep at every opportunity, and they had to keep waking me. The cool night refreshed me when I went to get the water from the well. Outside, it was quiet and empty. In the morning, the boss counted all the bread and again gave me only one loaf. I objected. Then he angrily added another loaf. Two loaves of bread were worth eighty rubles, while my monthly wages were one hundred rubles. I went straight to the market to sell the bread and see with my own eyes the eighty rubles I earned.

From then on, I was given two loaves of bread. We ate one and sold the other to buy necessities. With enough bread at home, a little money, and Mother's "payok," we could live. After coming home from work, I usually threw myself on the bed and fell asleep instantly. In the first month, whenever I finished work in the morning, I would sleep nearly all day and all night, and then I'd go back to work the following morning. I truly experienced the delight of this kind of sleep—rest. Under the German occupation, sleep was a kind of forgetting, and we waited for it all day. Now, I worked accompanied by the thought that I'd go home and go to sleep, but the reason was different: physical fatigue. How agreeable it was to think of sleeping at home when I was at work, all wet with water from dragging the leaking buckets to the bakery or, when, taking deep breaths, I kneaded the dough. Not that sleeping at home was all that luxurious. I dismantled several garden benches and built makeshift beds from them. But at the time, it seemed that in the entire world, there wasn't a more comfortable bed. After a month of such work, I was utterly exhausted. Mother's visit to my workplace nearly cost me a breakdown. I felt like a child and almost cried in front of her.

"It's better not to eat than for you to have to work so hard," Mother said. But I knew I would keep working. I couldn't expose my family to hunger; the bakery gave us bread, some money, and food rationing cards.

In the meantime, I quite unwittingly learned a bit of the tile-stove setter's craft. One day, we called a tile-stove setter to build us a stove. I watched him work and decided that I could do that too. When our neighbors' stove broke down, I had a chance to test my abilities. I offered to fix it and managed quite well. Soon people from the entire neighborhood came to me when they needed stove repairs. This gave me an extra income, which, combined with the two loaves of bread, became our material basis.

After two months of work at the bakery, I went to work for a different boss. There were three of us, and I became the boss's helper, no longer an apprentice. In this new capacity, I earned six loaves of bread. I brought them home, and my little sister sold them at the market. From then on, Mother bought daily half a kilogram of butter and the same amount of meat. I had to eat in order to maintain my strength. I earned more and more because at night we produced white bread from flour dust—of course only for our own use. This white bread brought a price six times higher than the regular bread that was rationed. I now earned six hundred or more rubles after twelve hours of work—the amount depended on whether the shift before stole any of our dough. On the other hand, our boss stole the dough belonging to the next shift, so in the end, no one was at a loss.

We earned our "profit" thus: Every now and then, we were given a new kind of flour. Then a test was performed to see how much bread this particular flour would yield. A baker from the outside was present at the first baking, and on the basis of the number of loaves of bread, he established the "norm" for each batch. During the testing, we always prepared the densest dough possible so that the fewest number of loaves would result. On the other hand, when we made the next batches, we diluted the dough as much as possible, to bake more loaves and keep the difference for ourselves. White bread was much more labor-intensive: we put several shovelfuls of flour into a sack and shook the sack until a white dust settled on the wooden tray for mixing the dough. We got several kilograms of white dust from an entire sack of flour, and with that, we baked one-kilogram loaves of white bread, which we then sold for a good price. It was no wonder that the "regular" bread, made mostly from husk and water, was of rather poor quality, and its crust didn't even hold.

In the end, the NKVD put its foot down because this business was going on in all the Wilno bakeries, not just in ours. Soon, several bakers were caught red-handed as they carried out the stolen loaves. From then on, we had to be extra careful. We found customers next to the bakery. In winter, I took the bread out on sleighs, just a few houses over, and I got the money right there. Before I carried out the "horses" (that was what the bakers called loaves of bread), I stepped outside to see whether anyone was watching.

As a result of these greater rigors, the bakers fondly remembered "the good old times of the German rule." Even though they kept their conversations secret from me because they didn't trust me as a Jew, I, nonetheless, understood from their whisperings that they interpreted the news as boding well for the Germans, and, in their imaginations, the Germans could be back in Wilno very soon. They linked this possibility with higher earnings and getting rid of the Soviets, whom they truly hated.

I could not fathom how someone could prefer the Germans to the Soviets. Soon enough, another apprentice, a young boy who likely was unaware of my origins, explained to me frankly that, "It's all because of the Jews, who run the whole show here." They preferred, then, to have the German whip over their heads than to deal with the few surviving Jews.

During my whole career as a baker, I had only one encounter with the NKVD. When I was coming home after work one night, someone jumped out of the house next door and shone a flashlight in my eyes: "Stoy," he said, "podydite somnoy" (halt; come up to me)." I had a bag in my hand with two loaves of bread. We walked a bit. I deliberated whether it would be a good idea to drop the bag surreptitiously. I thought that perhaps two loaves were enough evidence to get me arrested.

"Shto ti tom imeeyesh (what have you got there)?" he asked.

"Dve bulochki hleba … tovarishch, ya uchennik (two rolls of bread, comrade; I'm a student)," I answered.

"A bolshe nye imeeyesh (you don't have anything more)?" he asked and began to feel my clothes. "Nu, idzi domoy," he said at last, and let me go.

I was very lucky because another time he could have caught me with more bread, and who knows if a third loaf wouldn't have cost me my freedom.

On my way back home from the bakery, I always passed through a large square which, during the day, was a crowded marketplace, but at night, it was altogether empty and dark. One night when I was walking there, I suddenly heard a girl's voice calling my name, as if from underground. It was Sara Lewin, my friend from the Epsztajn Middle School. I recognized her at once: she had the same black braids I remembered, big black eyes, and she was short. She embraced and kissed me and then told me about two other classmates who survived with the partisans: Fisherovna and Pordominska. She invited me to come over—she lived nearby. I, however, was exhausted from work, and Mother was waiting impatiently for my return, so, regretfully, I had to turn down the invitation. I never saw her again, but I also never forgot that meeting.

Once I saw in the street Mr. Kowalski, my physics teacher from the Adam Mickiewicz Middle School. I spoke to him and found out that he had miraculously escaped death during the German occupation. He had a small locksmith workshop and did poorly, which was apparent from his haggard looks. Now and then I brought him some bread, for which I didn't take any money, even though he tried to pay me every time. I had always liked him and remembered his lessons as very pleasant.

One day, we received a telegram from our uncle in Moscow, informing us that Father was alive and well in Palestine. I found the telegram when I got home from work. Mother was still at the office, so I decided to go there directly to surprise her. I danced with my little sister and laughed out loud all the way there, without minding that people were turning their heads to watch us. I understood the importance of this piece of news: we again had a father, our caretaker, so we had to be happy. Father was in one piece in Palestine, the land of our ancestors. We must join him there; we must reach Palestine. That was our new goal. Everything would be easier to bear now since everything would bring us closer to him.

Mother kissed us all over when she heard the news. A new era of our life began. We were very eager to leave Wilno as soon as possible, especially since after a small delay, the Red Army was moving forward. Warsaw was free at last. Then the newspapers printed names of liberated towns on the way to Lodz. We applied to be repatriated to the temporary capital of Poland, Lublin. We wanted to be as close to Lodz as possible so that we could go there right after liberation. Lodz was free. We went to the Polish Patriots Committee every day to speed up our departure. Quite by accident, when I was fixing a stove in a house, I ran into my old Polish teacher, who was now an active and influential member of the Patriots Committee. That gave us the backing needed for a swift departure. We became friends with her, and she told us that she had helped to save many Jews during the war. She advised us not to admit to being Jewish in Poland and promised that it would make our life easier there because of rampant anti-Semitism. After a nerve-wracking wait, we saw our names on the list of passengers for repatriation train number three.

We made preparations for departure; we even sold Mother's coat to have a little money because we didn't want to be as penniless as we had been on arriving in Wilno. We bought a few kilograms of pork fat, and we brought along lots of bread and onions, knowing from experience that that was the best kind of food for the trip. Mother bought herself a cheap coat, which turned out to be a godsend later. I never thought that leaving my job would present any kind of a problem, but when I went to the main bakery office, I was told that I had to stay at work until a replacement was found. In the end, I left without anybody's permission, and in the morning, when I was supposed to be in the bakery, I was in one of the fifty cargo cars designated for repatriates.

There wasn't much room in the car. Several families, with their entire worldly possessions, took up almost all the space. We were crowded into a corner and could barely stretch. Only once the train was in motion, did I realize that there was a way to arrange the things so that there would be some free space. We did that together. The first two days and nights, we had only "dry rations" and the little bit to drink in the two thermoses we had brought along. Outside as well as inside, there was frost, so we slept in the clothes we were wearing.

Two days into the journey, we had our first longer stop. We cooked the first real meal of the trip, which everyone in the car devoured with great appetite. From that moment on, we were stopped more than we rode. In one place, the train was immobile for two days because the locomotive did not return. At the same station, we ran into people from repatriation train number two. There was a rumor that the main conductor of train number one had collected one hundred rubles from each passenger and bribed the station manager, who let the train depart. Most people wanted to follow this example, but a few were of the opinion that this would encourage the station master to expect bribes from all repatriation trains. We were very discouraged, annoyed, and tired. There was no indication of when we might depart. We wished to move forward, the way a traveler in the desert who has run out of water wants to get to an oasis.

When at last, on the third day, a locomotive was reattached, I was overjoyed; like a small child, I repeated: we're going to Lodz; we're going to Lodz. The train stopped at the border. We were prepared for a document control and a search and wanted to have this behind us, considering it to be the last obstacle on our way to Lodz and the beginning of a normal life. But there was no control, and, unexpectedly quickly, we moved on.

We were in Poland. Bialystok was the first large stop on the way. The ruined houses looked gloomy. Outside, there were Polish soldiers in long overcoats that looked bizarre because they were made according to the Russian model. The station was full of military trains with soldiers and equipment, which reminded me that the war was not over yet. We moved on.

The landscape became more vivid and more interesting, while the conversations in our car were less and less interesting. The main topic ever since we had left Wilno was ... the Jews. People discussed either political questions, which always led to the same conclusion: that all the ministers in the newly formed Polish government were Jews; or unending jokes combined with aping of the Jewish way of speaking. I wondered why these people never tired of the daily discussion on the same topic.

After ten days, the train arrived in Siedlce. From there, it was going to Lublin, so we had to get off, which we did happily. After a half-hour search at the Siedlce train station, we located a train filled with laborers returning from Germany to Warsaw and Prague. The cars were heated and spacious, and the passengers were less intelligent than the Wilno repatriates, and, perhaps for that reason, there was no talk of the Jews. We were as pleased as punch with everything, except for the presence of a young girl with a very swollen face; we feared that she might have erysipelas, or St. Anthony's fire, a very dangerous and contagious disease.

The laborers told us that the trains had been stopped for days in Siedlce. Fortunately for us, that very night, the provisions on the train ran out, and the train departed. Early the next morning, we were in Warszawa-Praga. From there we went to Lodz with two changes, in Koluszki and in Skierniewice. Each change meant a veritable struggle to get onto the next train with all of our luggage. Then the train arrived at the Kaliski Station in *Lodz*.

Photo after liberation
Part of Mother's ID as secretary in a weather station in Vilnius, 1945
At that time, the weather stations were under the
jurisdiction of the Interior Ministry of the Soviet Union

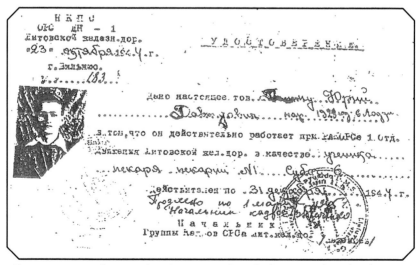

Document confirming that I am a student-baker in Railroad Bakery #1
October 1944, Vilnius

Główny Pełnomocnik
Polskiego Komitetu Wyzwolenia
Narodowego
15. *lutego* 1945r.

Zaświadczenie
dla ewakuacji do Polski

№ 5102

Okaziciel niniejszego **Dynin Jany**
(nazwisko, imię imię ojca)
s. Dawida

Rok urodzenia **1928**

Miejsce urodzenia **Łódź**

Narodowość **polska**

Ostatnie miejsce zamieszkania **Wilno Węgłowa 17**

Ewakuuje się do **Białegostoku** rejonu

wojewódtwa

Z nim ewakuują się:

Ważne do dnia **15 Marca** 1945 roku

Pełnomocnik Rejonowy do Spraw ewakuacji

Vałst. zp. „Varsan" 339/2500.

(podpis)

Document required to board the train leaving Wilno (Vilnius) to Poland
At that time, I was registered as being born in 1928;
the document above was issued by the Polish
Committee in Wilno on February 15, 1945

182

CHAPTER TEN

February 28, 1945

*Note: This chapter describes memories that
I wrote down on our return to Lodz.*

TODAY WE CAME HOME. At last we found ourselves at the Lodz train station. It was a strange feeling, as if nothing extraordinary had taken place. But I had yearned to be home so much, and I had imagined that when I arrived in Lodz, in my beloved Lodz, then for sure I would cry from the overwhelming emotion—which, I was convinced, would be sad. If only I could know that I would come home to Grandpa; that I'd find here my aunt and uncle, my beloved little cousin Majusia; that at the station we would be met by friends and relatives—wouldn't I have been counting the minutes till arrival?

But the conviction that no one would be there caused emptiness in my heart. Then I would think: *But maybe my intuition is wrong; maybe my beloved Grandpa is sitting on his balcony and will call out, "Fania, Jurek, Dzidzia! Thanks be to God!" And Mother will drop whatever she is carrying and will fly up to the second floor, to the apartment of her parents where she had spent her youth.*

Reality manifested itself to me soon enough. From the train station, we took a street car. I got off at the right stop, but Mother, by mistake, went one stop too far. Pulling our bundles behind me, I approached the apartment. Without waiting for Mother, I climbed the stairs. Oh, the number of times in my life that I had climbed these very stairs! At least as many as there had been Saturdays and holidays during our time in Lodz. I reached the landing; I threw down my bundles, and I walked up to the door. The name plate said: Ignacy Wawrzyniak. I did not give up, but it could not be possible. I rang the bell. An older woman opened the door.

"Is Mr. Glowinski in?" I asked, almost in a whisper.

"And who is that?" she asked in return.

Tears came to my eyes.

March 26, 1945: From a letter to my father:

Father, spring has come. It's warm, and soon everything will be green. When we came here, there was still frost that we survived in an unheated apartment. Nothing has changed in Lodz; there are no new buildings. You can imagine with what tension I climbed up the stairs of the house at 85 Zeromskiego Street, the home of Grandpa and Grandma. Unfortunately, a stranger opened the door. No one we knew was there. There is still a tiny bit of hope that perhaps they had been taken from the camp to Germany, but we can't count on that. We will have more detailed news of the family when we meet with Cousin Rachel, who survived in Warsaw. Our life is slowly becoming settled. Mother works at the Voivodship office. I'm in the second year of Lyceum, that is, I will be taking my final high-school exam this year. I cannot imagine how I will do that because all knowledge has evaporated from my head, but I'm not worried. The Jewish committee gives us some bread and other food, but it's not enough. In our apartment on Kosciuszki Avenue, we found all the furniture in the bedroom, dining room, and my room. In the living room, your desk and the soft armchairs were missing. Whoever had left our furniture also left behind so much trash that it took me days to clean up. As for antiques and paintings, the Kraut who was living here took them somewhere near Vienna, but we don't know exactly where. If we had returned a bit earlier, we would have probably found more things in place, as much must have been plundered after the liberation. If you were here with us, the matter of getting our things back would look differently, but we are exhausted after everything we have been through. Only Jadzia, our former servant, returned a bit of our linens and some china to us. There is no trace of the dining service. Grandma had given their things to some janitor whose identity was not known to us. Jadzia also brought us back our photographs and other souvenirs. The most important thing is that we're alive and even more important is that we'll see you soon … It's the Sunday before Easter; Passover is coming, and we don't have any food. Last year at this time, we were still under the yoke of the "super bandits," and now we are free. The curse of death is gone, but there are moments when we don't believe it. Three years were a horrible nightmare that has left its trace in us and in human psyche as such. Each passing day was a miracle, and for us, there were over a thousand such days. We were surrounded by blood and betrayal. Every human being who has any excuse for the Germans is worthy of sharing their fate. Their fate must be torture and then the gallows, and that's why I ask you, Father, to oppress these "supermen" whenever you have a chance, if only to avenge the barbaric death of your mother and all the mothers, your brother Jona and all the brothers. They are not people, but bandits. The world will breathe more freely when the last man of this cursed race will disappear from the Earth. Dear Father, I hope that war will end soon, and we will see each other. Do not forget about us who are your family, and remember that it's a great MIRACLE that we are alive. Your son, Jerzy.

April 20, 1945

Today Rachel Szyk, our cousin on Father's side, came to see us. We saw the naked truth. Our relatives are dead. In fact, this is only a confirmation of what we already knew, but we still lived with the illusion that perhaps someone had survived. From what she told us, it seems that the first to perish was little Majusia, that angel of a girl. I can still see her blue eyes and her golden hair. Can it be true that this holy, untouched wonder stopped breathing, that her young lungs were filled with the murderous gas? Can it be true that her beautiful hair was used to fill the mattress of some German who bought it for a few Deutsch marks? No, this must be a bad dream. She could not have died: a little baby girl, like those in holy pictures. Nonetheless, she went to her death in Treblinka, along with her grandmother. For what? So that some German could sit on a sofa stuffed with her hair and with the hair of her mother or her grandmother.

May 8, 1945

The war has ended. We should be jumping for joy, but instead we are calm, as if nothing unusual were happening. Sirens started the war, and sirens end it. I can still hear their sound on September 1, 1939, when the war began. Five years and eight months later, these sirens are music to our ears. A new era is beginning. It will be the era of welfare for all the just nations and the era of atonement for all the nations in the grips of racial hatred and pride. A new life will begin for me, a life for which millions of others have sacrificed their lives. Humanity has not known such losses. The Jewish nation has suffered the most. Homage to the heroes! We must be happy; the horrific nightmare is gone. But the heart is heavy with the knowledge of the cost …

August 7, 1945

As of yesterday, your son has passed the final high-school exam. Yesterday was the last day of the oral exams, after which the principal read the list of the students who passed; my name was on it. Dear Father, I don't wish to boast, but this is a real feat after years of not opening a single book: years when we only thought of survival; when we trembled every minute, or rather, every second; when we had to work hard and steal hard, and we lived in constant terror; when there was no time for study, and all the knowledge I had acquired earlier evaporated without a trace. When I arrived in Lodz and entered middle school, it seemed to me that it would be a total waste of time. All that had been simple before became impenetrable for my head. After a month of study, the situation improved, then it went pretty well, and then … the final exams. There are moments, however, when the depression caused by many years of slavery and of struggle to survive makes me feel quite indifferent about having passed these exams. It is a surprise even to me how indifferent I have become to everything around me. It is hard to live without any friends or relatives. Just think, how would you react; how would you feel in such a desert? Do you understand? The thought of you is our only salvation. Will these words reach you? Will you be able to share in our joy that your son has passed his final high-school exam? I don't know, but I believe that sooner or later, in a month or two, our family will be able to celebrate an even greater kind of holiday: our reunion after the long separation. Your son, Jerzy.

October 26, 1945: From a letter to my father:

It would be a sin to complain. And yet emptiness lies in our hearts. It is as if we were at some train station on the way to you. Can you understand it? While I write this, the radio is playing first-rate jazz. But even that doesn't make me happy. We almost never go to the cinema because we lack the patience to sit through the entire film … We lead a very modest life. This is all the easier since we had a three-year "practice." And it is this "practice" that puts us in this mood … Thus the night has passed, one of the one thousand and a half nights of your separation from your family. Night was always a blessing for us. At night during the occupation, we always felt calm. We spent the whole day waiting for dusk. Occasionally, a fantastic dream would give us back our relatives and friends, at least for a few minutes: normal times, you. After such a dream came the waking, terrifying in its reality, and the question: will we live till the next night? And so the days went by, until the moment of liberation, preceded by homelessness and the front. We were liberated in the middle of a forest, where we were hiding from the Germans and from the front. The patrol that came to free us was one of the signs heralding our eventual meeting with you. I will admit, though, that we were not thinking of you at the time, that was how preoccupied we were with ourselves. That patrol was the border between our death and life. We were entering life ... Your son, Jerzy.

Our journey from Poland to Eretz Israel

November 27, 1945

The first stage of our road to Eretz Israel was Szczecin, where we were put up for a few days in a house rented just for that purpose. It was far from the center of the city so that no one would see such a large group of people with suitcases, which could have tipped off the police. Then we crossed the border into Western Germany without much difficulty, and we reached the suburbs of Berlin.

Berlin. The car stopped some two hundred meters from the sign that said "Berlin." This was a suburb, about a dozen kilometers away from the center of the city. We didn't continue by car because an open truck filled with people and luggage would have been too noticeable … Once we emerged from the station of the metro, we still had to pass many houses, some whole and some in ruins, in a dark street. We finally made it to the gate of the house at 28 Oranienburg, the headquarters of the Jewish committee. We thought that by coming into that house, we were entering a safe and quiet haven …

December 19, 1945. From a letter to my father:

Dear Father, we have been in Berlin for over two weeks now, and there are no official possibilities of continuing further. We will go on by smuggling ourselves through the border between West and East Germany. It's hard, but I'm not losing the hope that we will spend the holidays together. Kisses, Jurek.

January 21, Hannover

Before we made it here, we "saw all the stars." I was so feeble that my nose bled several times a day, and I could barely see. You can imagine Mother's state. Dzidzia made it in one piece. I carried her and her big backpack most of the way. When she walked, she would fall into deep holes with snow, and I had to pull her out just as we were crossing the heavily patrolled border between West and East Germany. Our guides were local Germans, who had been submarine crewmembers during the war. Every day of our stay here helps us regain our strength, and we are almost back to normal. We live comfortably, and the dear UNRA furnishes us with everything that we need. I send you springtime greetings. My dream is to be with you as soon as possible. I'm terribly behind in the study of foreign languages, sports, and health, but I'm convinced this can be remedied in a matter of months. I'm curious about the youth life in Eretz Israel. Any pretty girls there?

Having received the official exit visas, called certificates, we left Hannover on a direct train: Hamburg to Brussels. After a few pleasant days in the latter city, we went to Paris. That was where I met Annette.

From a letter to Annette:

Annette, it's a pity that you're so far away from me. I consider you a friend, just as we have agreed in the beautiful Ville d'Avray. I believe that you will be happy and wish you this happiness with all my heart. To ensure that it comes about, I will make a wish upon a falling star. It's supposed to come true …

Our route led through Marseille, where we boarded the seventy-ton ship *Andre Lebon.*

From a letter to Annette:

We went by way of Tunis and Egypt. On the first day, sea sickness emptied the dining hall. Every couple of minutes, another passenger left the table, covering his or her mouth with a hand. I thought it very funny, until at dessert I, too, began to feel as if I were going to follow in their footsteps. I didn't go all the way, but had to give up the last course. We approached Bizerte. It's a smallish town, situated at the bottom of a large mountain. The houses on the shore were in ruins; the war has left its traces here as well. The locals in their red fezzes were a novelty to me. I had never seen anything like that. The place where our ship came to shore was filled with a company of colorful soldiers who chased their brothers away from the ship. The French helped them along, and the only difference between them and their mercenaries was that the French were more brutal. Here I saw, for the first time, the European violence against the dark-skinned people. This violence caused a certain reaction of compassion on our ship, and people began to whistle, myself included. The most interesting custom of this harbor was the "throwing of fruit." The locals purposefully bought fruit from the port vendors and then threw the fruit to us on the ship. Most of it, however, hit the ship's side and fell into the sea or smashed on board into an inedible mass. From the ship, people threw money—francs. Oranges and apricots, so much desired, fell on our heads. Such were my first impressions of Africa: a hospitable welcome with fruit. After a few more days of seafaring, we arrived at a harbor that greeted us with the smell of onion and rotten eggs: Alexandria. The Egyptian police immediately "took care" of us. They were on the ship minutes after our arrival, and three more police boats were circling the ship. Many passengers were supposed to go ashore in Alexandria. Following the police, many small private boats appeared, and their owners began fighting for passengers. Our ship was a few hundred meters from the shore. The system worked as follows: a passenger would have his luggage snatched away from him and would therefore be forced to follow. Some passengers found themselves in a difficult situation: their suitcases were in three different boats, and they themselves in a fourth. I'm sure that it took a lot of effort to put it all together on shore. It was only in the evening that the ship made fast at the quay. The crowd of locals on the quay seemed very original to me. Red fezzes, white turbans, long robes, rags next to the fancy clothing of other Egyptians—all this composed a curious mosaic. Among them bustled the vendors of fruit juice, carrying huge jugs over their shoulders. They looked all the more interesting because they had large copper plates which they banged against each other to draw the attention of their customers. The port workers look wretched: dirty, hungry, emaciated. I watched their work closely and noticed that they were chanting while pulling their loads, and that the moment of greatest effort coincided with the accent. Next to them walk their Egyptian brothers, dressed in beautiful European clothes, doing nothing, and looking apathetically into the distance. At lunch time, the workers would buy food consisting of a pancake filled with tomatoes and other treats, which the vendor then sprinkled with some liquid from a bottle, at the "moveable bars."

At last, we came to the final stage of our journey. We were near the Suez Canal. From the distance, I could see the light of a lighthouse: Port Said.

We arrived in Haifa in the morning, and the ship was met by many motor boats. I watched the faces carefully. *Is Father on one of them? Perhaps he has changed so much that I can't recognize him?* I looked around intensely, but I had a feeling that he was not in the harbor. A man walked up to us, asking for our last name. He informed us that Father had to leave for Italy for two weeks on business, but should be back soon. I clench my teeth in order not to explode, and I calmed Mother down. After a few minor formalities, we got onto the motor boat with the luggage.

May 24, 1946, at 10 a.m., we set foot on land. We entered the Holy Land; if we did not love it yet, we would have to get to love it, because only this earth could soothe us after all the years of struggle for life, when the death shroud seemed to be above our heads at all times.

Written after arrival at Father's:

Where am I?

I'm dreaming: Tel-Aviv, Eretz Israel, my Father.

I'm dreaming. This is only a dream because the year is really 1943. Tremble, all who behold these numbers.

They contain millions of killed people, millions of others imprisoned behind the barbed wires of the concentration camps.

I'm not dreaming. This is one huge prison; you fear for your life at every moment; you regret your life; you're young. You want to live.

"Why do they want to kill me, what for?" you keep asking yourself, and you find no answer. Our nation is doomed, you think.

You call out to God, "Help! Where are You? Help!"

You are certain that God will not abandon you, but you tremble, nonetheless. And if there isn't …

He *is*, without *him* I wouldn't know how to survive even for a moment.

He helped you, without *him* there was no hope because none of our hopes were based on anything real; they relied on a *miracle*.

"Where am I?" I ask myself.

Do I live on the earth? Is this some kind of a dream? Will I wake up all of a sudden, and again it will be 1942 or 1943 …

Oh, how I had waited for such a dream; those were my moments of oblivion, dreams, and day dreams. I lived in dreams.

How modest they were, how innocent, how bright.

I saw myself in these dreams as a savior: a savior from all evil, at my own expense.

People, can you understand this? Do you understand where I am now, and where I was?

I myself don't understand this; this is incomprehensible; one could go mad just by trying to understand it at once. It is so strange and unreal.

Where am I?

From a letter to Ninka, written already in Eretz Israel—a letter sent to Poland:

If I miss anything of nature, it is the forest. I never miss the snow. Here I must transport myself back to the not-so-very-distant war times in order to make you—and myself—realize why I give precisely this answer. Snow means winter: the cemetery of the poor, the abandoned, the pursued, the persecuted. That was what things were like where I was at the time, in Belarus. Can we be allowed to sigh to snow, to its fluffiness, whiteness, to its beautiful microscopic structure? Snow meant that the traces of the people running away from the German hatred were visible, and the pursuit made easy. Is it permissible to yearn after the frost, the gravedigger of the enfeebled and the homeless, roaming the fields and the woods … We mustn't think of snow the way it was before the war; the snow we used for snowball fights after we came out of our warm apartments, bundled up in warm clothes by our parents. That snow does not exist for us any longer. We remember the "bad" snow and instinctively ask, "Can this happen again?"

Lodz. It was a foreign city, foreign streets. From the apartments made dear to us by memories, strange and hateful people peered at us and told us directly that it was a shame we had survived. People who like polyps sat on the hearths that had belonged to our family, people who wanted to erect a monument to Hitler for having given them this possibility of plunder ... Can you forget the loss of your loved ones, of your classmates? Has their memory not remained in your mind? Does the knowledge that *they are not there* not chase you from that cemetery?

EPILOGUE

UNFORTUNATELY, I COULDN'T RENDER the real nature of our experience, for I described the dark moments in such a manner that they almost counterbalance the bright ones in the years under the occupation. The uncertainty of tomorrow was a dark moment that never truly left us, oppressing us mercilessly, but I could describe it only here and there. In fact, this was the factor that made torture out of several years of our lives.

Before I finish these memoirs, I must mention something that I promised myself one night in Horodyszcze: to describe that night.

It's night. Outside the moon is shining. The telephone wires play a monotonous melody. The street is empty. Frost bites my cheeks. I carry the remnants of the chopped firewood to the room. I close the shutters. Now I can go to sleep. Sleep is the greatest delight. But first, an infinite prayer. Amen.

It is now 7:15 p.m. I'm in Athens, Georgia. The date is September 28, 2002: I just finished transcribing what I wrote so many years ago.

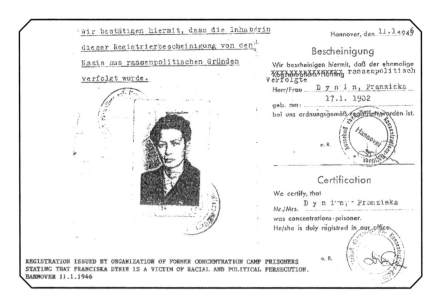

Certificate from the City of Berlin, asking help for me to travel without difficulties to München (Munich); we actually traveled to Hannover
Reflecting my Polish documents, the certificate
states that I was born in 1929
Berlin, December 18, 1945

REGISTRATION ISSUED BY ORGANIZATION OF FORMER CONCENTRATION CAMP PRISONERS STATING THAT FRANCISKA DYNIN IS A VICTIM OF RACIAL AND POLITICAL PERSECUTION. HANNOVER 11.1.1946

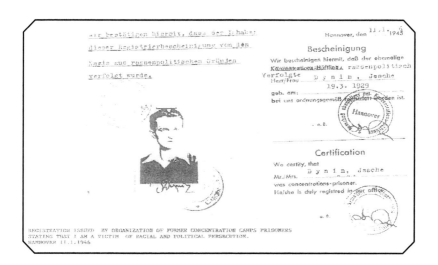

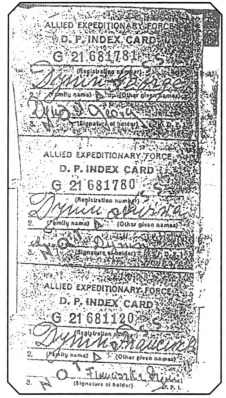

Displaced Persons Index Cards, issued to our family by
the authorities in the British Zone in Germany

Photo made in Paris (probably for a document)

Sketch of me by my friend, Annette, from Ville d'Avray, France

AFTERWORD

MY THOUGHTS ABOUT *ARYAN PAPERS*

It was written "just like it was," without any consideration of how it would be judged by others. The events took place over six decades ago, and I wrote it down soon after liberation to the best of my ability and recollection.

Nothing was added and nothing was deleted to satisfy anybody. It is not a novel but the facts about how it was and how we were.

Even at the time I was writing, in 1946-47, I was already a completely changed person. Therefore, it was even more difficult to relive the past and to write *Aryan Papers* in the way I wrote it.

George Dynin

ADDENDUM

*Official history of Gorodysce (Gorodishche), the
part relating to the German Occupation until
liberation (July 24, 1941–June 8, 1944)*

Translated from Belorussian:

ON JULY 24, 1941, German forces entered the town of Gorodishche. From June 24, 1941, until July, 8, 1944, Gorodishche was occupied by fascist invaders. From the first day of occupation, "the new order" was established. In the town, the fifty-seventh punitive battalion was accommodated. The leader of this battalion was Major Zigling. The commandant of Gorodishche was Lieutenant Klyatz, and the head of the gendarmerie was master Ganik.

Before the Second World War, Gorodishche had a large number of Jewish and Polish citizens, but it was these people who were most affected by the new fascist order. In the fall of 1941, mass executions of Jews began. On October 20, 1941, Germans gathered around one hundred Jewish men on the pretext of building new defensive works and led them with shovels to dig holes in the forest of Mihnovshchina and village of Pogoreltzy. As soon as the work was finished, all of the Jewish men were executed at the same place. On July 21 and 22, 1941, fascists gathered all Jewish people in Gorodishche near a local church. Some of them were driven, some were led on foot, to the forest of Mihnovshchina and village of Pogoreltzy (two kilometers from Gorodishche), where all were executed. Among them was a Rabbi Morduhovich (105 years old), a hairdresser Elin, two brothers named Krasilshchik, and others.

Sixty-eight Jews were locked in a ghetto in Gorodishche on Slonimsk Street. It was here they also sent all those who had previously escaped and were hiding in villages nearby. In the beginning of May 1942, thirty-five people from the ghetto were shot near the church in Gorodishche.

In August 1942, one hundred Jews were executed near the orthodox cemetery. In November 1942, one hundred Gypsies were shot at the same place. On October 21, 1941, fascists collected seventy people: teachers, doctors, lawyers. They all were executed in the forest Mihnovshchina.

In March 1942, Victor Koltzov (a doctor, a prisoner of war), Vladimir Ivanov (a lieutenant of Red Army, a prisoner of war), Ivan Smirnov (a prisoner of war) were executed near the orthodox church in Gorodishche.

In the spring of 1942, a major from the Red Army (his name remains unknown) and Sergeant Ivan Kolesov were tortured and killed. They were buried behind the church in Gorodishche.

In May 1944, on the square in Gorodishche, members of Komsomol, from the villages of Girmantovtzy, Kuptzevuch, Reshetnik, and Sheyna were hanged for their connection with partisan groups and antifascist activity. Their bodies hung for three days; the Germans did not allow their parents to bury them.

In the summer of 1942, in Gorodishche near a church, a Jewish woman named Morduh was shot, along with two children. She went mad on the way to the place of execution.

In May and June 1944, the fifty-seventh punitive battalion arrested one hundred and fifty Polish people. They all were sent to the concentration camp in Koldyczewo and brutally killed.

Excavation and examination of the graves at the Koldyczewo camp showed that the majority of corpses had signs of brutal tortures. Hands of corpses were tied with barbed wire.

During the years of occupation, 4,006 people from Gorodishche were executed.

On May 2, 1943, the village of Zastarinye was surrounded by the fifty-seventh punitive battalion from Gorodishche. The whole population, regardless of sex or age, was driven together into the houses (fifteen or twenty people in each), where they were made to lie on the floor with their faces down, and they were executed. After that, each house was burned. A total of 382 people were killed and ninety-six houses were burned.

Pelageya Iosifovna Lenko (seventy years old, from the village Yalutzevichi), having survived by chance told: "When the fascists came from Gorodishche to Zastarinye, I was on the street. They pushed me into the house of Fursa. There were eighteen or twenty people in the house, including children of different ages. They made us lie on the floor, and after that they began to shoot us. When everything was over, I, wounded, saw the child of Vasiliy Danilevich, who was two months old. His head was broken, probably from the hit of the wall; his body was torn in half."

During the occupation, 3,427 people of different nationalities also were executed in the town of Gorodishche.

In the concentration camp in Koldyczewo, 22,000 people from Gorodishche and other regions of Baranovichi district were executed.

The Germans also transported to Germany 573 men and women during the occupation.

(All the information is taken from a document of the Gorodishche Committee considering the cases of execution and transportation of Soviet people by fascists on the territory of the Gorodishche Region, Baranovichi District from 1941 to 1944. This document is dated April 23, 1945.)

But people did not give up. More than a thousand residents of the Gorodishche region fought the enemy.

There were organized, secret district committees of KP/b/B and

LKSMB, partisan groups named "Twenty-five years to Belarus," "The Suvorov group," "Pervomayskaya." There was also an edited newspaper "Partisan of Belarus." Partisans derailed hundreds of trains, destroyed hundreds of kilometers of rails, and killed thousands of Nazis.

On June 8, 1944, Gorodishche was freed by the army of the First Belorussian Front.

At the present time, Gorodishche is the main regional town. The population is 2,490 people. Their occupations are agriculture, education, culture, trade, service, transportation, and others. There is a big bakery, town hospital, high school, music and sport schools, day-care, library, and orphanage.

The Assistant of the Chief of the Region
Committee, Baranovichi, Belarus
L. I. Hrenovsky

Photos from the time of my service in the Israeli Army (Signal Corps 1948-1951)

Photo from "Burma Road" on the way to Jerusalem. During the War of Independence, this was the single road to Jerusalem that was open to bring supplies to this city. The American Colonel Marcus was in charge of this operation. He was killed on June 11, 1948, by friendly fire.

Photo taken by my friend; place unknown

Photo for military ID

Photos from Israel after the war was over

With my parents and sister in a coffee house in Tel-Aviv

With my sister on the shore in Herzliya

Afternoon on the patio of the Sharon Hotel in Herzliya

Visit to an ancient aqueduct

Afternoon ride in Yarkon Park

Rowing on the Yarkon River

With my mother and sister at the home of my parents on Shderot Chen Street, Tel-Aviv, 1997

דוד דינין   פניה דינין

בן משה   בת לאון

נפ' ט"ו אייר תשמ"ח   נפ' ט"ו כסלו תש"ס

1898 - 1985

The final resting place of my parents

*The last photo of my mother before she passed
away at the age of ninety-eight*

*My father during WWII in the Polish Army. After the so-called
"Amnesty," he was able to join General Anders' Army. The
units of this army were active in the Middle East and Italy.*

*A reunion of my old schoolmates in the home
of my sister, Herzliya Pituach, 1999
From left to right: me, Julek Alpern, Mietek Rosen, Tolek
Lichtenstein; absent from the photo is Sevek Erlich
All of us were in the same class in a school in Lodz
(Gimnazjum Spoleczne) before the war; Mietek, Tolek,
and I also attended kindergarten before attending the
Gimnazjum Spoleczne. From a class of about thirty Jewish
students, we survived to meet each other in Israel.*

*Inscribed on this plaque is the first line of my poem "Holocaust"
Savannah, Georgia, April 1998*

Standing next to the Memorial
Savannah, Georgia, May 1998

The hero of WWII Jan Karski
The famous Righteous Gentile was the guest in our home in Savannah
My wife, Marlene, and I are on either side of him

Marlene and me next to our home in Athens, Georgia, 2002

*As a visiting lecturer on the Holocaust in the
Department of Comparative Literature, the University
of Georgia. Athens, Georgia, 2002*

*On September 6, 2004, the "Brigadier General, Count Kasimir Pulaski–
Captain Alexander O'Neil, Department of the Army, United States of
America Medal & Award of Merit" was bestowed upon George Dynin*

ABOUT THE AUTHOR

GEORGE DYNIN was born in Lodz, Poland, in 1925. He, his mother, and his sister survived the Holocaust by living on false documents. In 1946, they were reunited with George's father in Tel-Aviv. George served in the Israeli Army during the War of Independence in 1948. He moved to the U.S. in 1958 and started an import/export company. He lives with his wife in Athens, Georgia, giving lectures at various schools, churches, and events.

INDEX

CPSIA information can be obtained at www.ICGtesting.com
Printed in the USA
LVOW08s2017171014

409267LV00001B/18/P

9 781480 811379